The Sheldon
Book of Verse

COMPILED BY

P. G. SMITH

AND

J. F. WILKINS

II

OXFORD UNIVERSITY PRESS

Oxford University Press, Ely House, London W. 1

GLASGOW NEW YORK TORONTO MELBOURNE WELLINGTON
CAPE TOWN SALISBURY IBADAN NAIROBI LUSAKA ADDIS ABABA
BOMBAY CALCUTTA MADRAS KARACHI LAHORE DACCA
KUALA LUMPUR SINGAPORE HONG KONG TOKYO

FIRST PUBLISHED 1957

REPRINTED LITHOGRAPHICALLY IN GREAT BRITAIN
AT THE UNIVERSITY PRESS, OXFORD
FROM SHEETS OF THE FIRST EDITION
1962, 1969

PREFACE

THE perfect anthology is one that contains *all* the poems you really like; but if you are fortunate enough to care greatly for poetry, it might require special transport. Some volumes, less ambitious, nevertheless, have established their hold on the affections: *The Oxford Book of English Verse*, even if it dies (in effect) at Swinburne; *The Golden Treasury*, battered but handy, in many a travelling bag; Walter de la Mare's *Come Hither*, which mingles quiet music with amiably irrelevant notes, without ever losing the true thread of poetry; or General Wavell's unpretentiously titled *Other Men's Flowers*. Some of these may claim to have been representative collections of English poetry; but they hold their place, in fact, by some virtue of choice or of spirit.

The aim of *The Sheldon Book of Verse* is more limited, in the sense that the four volumes are planned as a graded course for use in schools up to the fifth form. But they contain enough poems for private reading as well as for class use, and we hope that the variety of choice and arrangement may encourage the reader to browse in them, so that they may become more than mere textbooks. We have tried to give a widely representative selection of the older poets while putting a strong emphasis on modern poetry; more than two-fifths of the poems are copyright ones. Each book contains several poems of a length unusual in anthologies, and some poems which may tax the reader's understanding and appreciation, together with poems by American authors, and a selection of light verse. The emphasis varies according

3

to the book: Books I and II contain more narrative verse and strongly marked rhythms and images, while from Books III to IV there is a transition to more philosophical verse, or love poetry.

The poems are arranged, not in rigid groups by subject-matter, but so that one leads to another along some thread of similarity or contrast, which may depend upon mood, subject, style, form, age, or authorship.

To facilitate more formal study, there are brief notes at the end and indexes which may suggest a grouping of poems by subject, period, style, and so on.

If this anthology succeeds in giving pleasure, in opening for its readers a way to the enjoyment and appreciation of poetry, it will have achieved its aim.

P. G. S.
J. F. W.

Taunton
December, 1958

ACKNOWLEDGEMENTS

Mr. Martin Armstrong and Messrs. A. D. Peters for 'Miss Thompson goes Shopping'.

Messrs. Gerald Duckworth Ltd. for 'Jim' from *Cautionary Tales* and 'The Hippopotamus' from *The Bad Child's Book of Beasts* by Hilaire Belloc.

Messrs. A. D. Peters and the Belloc Estate for 'Tarantella' by Hilaire Belloc.

Messrs. Methuen & Co. Ltd. for 'Stage Directions' from *Harlem and Other Poems* by W. R. Benet.

Messrs. Sidgwick & Jackson Ltd. for 'The Great Lover' by Rupert Brooke.

Miss Dorothy Collins and Messrs. Methuen Ltd. for 'The Rolling English Road' from *The Collected Poems of G. K. Chesterton*.

The Executors of John Davidson and The Richards Press for 'A Runnable Stag' by John Davidson.

Mrs. H. M. Davies and Messrs. Jonathan Cape Ltd. for 'The Kingfisher' from *The Collected Poems of W. H. Davies*.

Mr. A. T. A. Dobson, as representing the Executors, and the Oxford University Press for 'Ballad to Queen Elizabeth' by Austin Dobson.

Messrs. J. M. Dent & Co. Ltd. for 'War Song of the Saracens' by J. E. Flecker.

Mr. Wilfred Gibson and Messrs. Macmillan & Co. for 'The Ice Cart' and 'Flannan Isle'.

Messrs. Edward Arnold Ltd. for 'Lord Gorbals' from *More Ruthless Rhymes* by Harry Graham.

The Trustees of the Hardy Estate and Messrs. Macmillan & Co. Ltd. for 'The Oxen' and 'When I set out for Lyonnesse' from *The Collected Poems of Thomas Hardy*.

Mr. Ralph Hodgson and Messrs. Macmillan & Co. Ltd. for 'The Bull' from *Poems*.

CONTENTS

From *The Great Lover*

THESE I have loved:
      White plates and cups, clean-gleaming,
Ringed with blue lines; and feathery, faery dust;
Wet roofs, beneath the lamp-light; the strong crust
Of friendly bread; and many-tasting food;
Rainbows; and the blue bitter smoke of wood;
And radiant raindrops couching in cool flowers;
And flowers themselves, that sway through sunny hours,
Dreaming of moths that drink them under the moon;
Then, the cool kindliness of sheets, that soon
Smooth away trouble; and the rough male kiss
Of blankets; grainy wood; live hair that is
Shining and free; blue-massing clouds; the keen
Unpassioned beauty of a great machine;
The benison of hot water; furs to touch;
The good smell of old clothes; and other such—
The comfortable smell of friendly fingers,
Hair's fragrance, and the musty reek that lingers
About dead leaves and last year's ferns. . . .

                          Dear names,
And thousand other throng to me! Royal flames;
Sweet water's dimpling laugh from tap or spring;
Holes in the ground; and voices that do sing;
Voices in laughter, too; and body's pain,
Soon turned to peace; and the deep-panting train;
Firm sands; the little dulling edge of foam
That browns and dwindles as the wave goes home;
And washen stones, gay for an hour; the cold
Graveness of iron; moist black earthen mould;

Sleep; and high places; footprints in the dew;
And oaks; and brown horse-chestnuts, glossy-new;
And new-peeled sticks; and shining pools on grass;—
All these have been my loves.

RUPERT BROOKE

2

Adlestrop

YES. I remember Adlestrop—
The name, because one afternoon
Of heat the express-train drew up there
Unwontedly. It was late June.

The steam hissed. Some one cleared his throat.
No one left and no one came
On the bare platform. What I saw
Was Adlestrop—only the name

And willows, willow-herb, and grass,
And meadowsweet, and haycocks dry,
No whit less still and lonely fair
Than the high cloudlets in the sky.

And for that minute a blackbird sang
Close by, and round him, mistier,
Farther and farther, all the birds
Of Oxfordshire and Gloucestershire.

EDWARD THOMAS

3   *The Lake Isle of Innisfree*

I WILL arise and go now, and go to Innisfree,
And a small cabin build there, of clay and wattles made:
Nine bean rows will I have there, a hive for the honey-bee,
   And live alone in the bee-loud glade.

And I shall have some peace there, for peace comes dropping
     slow,
Dropping from the veils of the morning to where the cricket
     sings;
There midnight's all a glimmer, and noon a purple glow,
   And evening full of the linnet's wings.

I will arise and go now, for always night and day
I hear lake water lapping with low sounds by the shore;
While I stand on the roadway, or on the pavements grey,
   I hear it in the deep heart's core.

W. B. YEATS

4   *The Ice-cart*

PERCHED on my city office-stool
I watched with envy while a cool
And lucky carter handled ice. . . .
And I was wandering in a trice
Far from the grey and grimy heat
Of that intolerable street
O'er sapphire berg and emerald floe
Beneath the still, cold ruby glow
Of everlasting Polar night,
Bewildered by the queer half-light,

Until I stumbled unawares
Upon a creek where big white bears
Plunged headlong down with flourished heels
And floundered after shining seals
Through shivering seas of blinding blue.
And, as I watched them, ere I knew,
I'd stripped and I was swimming, too,
Among the seal-pack, young and hale,
And thrusting on with threshing tail,
With twist and twirl and sudden leap
Through crackling ice and salty deep,
Diving and doubling with my kind
Until at last we left behind
Those big white blundering bulks of death,
And lay at length with panting breath
Upon a far untravelled floe,
Beneath a gentle drift of snow—
Snow drifting gently, fine and white,
Out of the endless Polar night,
Falling and falling evermore
Upon that far untravelled shore,
Till I was buried fathoms deep
Beneath that cold white drifting sleep—
Sleep drifting deep,
Deep drifting sleep. . . .

The carter cracked a sudden whip:
I clutched my stool with startled grip,
Awakening to the grimy heat
Of that intolerable street.

W. W. GIBSON

From *The Deserted Village*

EVENING

SWEET was the sound, when oft at evening's close
Up yonder hill the village murmur rose;
There, as I passed with careless steps and slow,
The mingling notes came softened from below;
The swain responsive as the milk-maid sung,
The sober herd that lowed to meet their young;
The noisy geese that gabbled o'er the pool,
The playful children just let loose from school;
The watchdog's voice that bayed the whisp'ring wind,
And the loud laugh that spoke the vacant mind:
These all in sweet confusion sought the shade,
And filled each pause the nightingale had made.

THE SCHOOLMASTER

BESIDE yon straggling fence that skirts the way,
With blossomed furze unprofitably gay,
There, in his noisy mansion, skilled to rule,
The village master taught his little school;
A man severe he was, and stern to view,
I knew him well, and every truant knew;
Well had the boding tremblers learned to trace
The day's disasters in his morning face;
Full well they laughed with counterfeited glee
At all his jokes, for many a joke had he;
Full well the busy whisper, circling round,
Conveyed the dismal tidings when he frowned;
Yet he was kind, or, if severe in aught,
The love he bore to learning was in fault;

The village all declared how much he knew;
'Twas certain he could write, and cypher too;
Lands he could measure, terms and tides presage,
And even the story ran that he could gauge;
In arguing too, the parson owned his skill,
For e'en though vanquished, he could argue still;
While words of learned length and thundering sound
Amazed the gazing rustics ranged around,
And still they gazed, and still the wonder grew,
That one small head could carry all he knew.

OLIVER GOLDSMITH

6   *Miss Thompson goes Shopping*

In her lone cottage on the downs,
With winds and blizzards and great crowns
Of shining cloud, with wheeling plover
And short grass sweet with the small white clover,
Miss Thompson lived, correct and meek,
A lonely spinster, and every week
On market-day she used to go
Into the little town below,
Tucked in the great downs' hollow bowl
Like pebbles gathered in a shoal.

So, having washed her plates and cup
And banked the kitchen-fire up,
Miss Thompson slipped upstairs and dressed,
Put on her black (her second best),
The bonnet trimmed with rusty plush,
Peeped in the glass with simpering blush,
From camphor-smelling cupboard took
Her thicker jacket off the hook

Because the day might turn to cold.
Then, ready, slipped downstairs and rolled
The hearthrug back: then searched about,
Found her basket, ventured out,
Snecked the door and paused to lock it
And plunge the key in some deep pocket.
Then as she tripped demurely down
The steep descent, the little town
Spread wider till its sprawling street
Enclosed her and her footfalls beat
On hard stone pavement, and she felt
Those throbbing ecstasies that melt
Through heart and mind, as, happy, free,
Her small, prim personality
Merged into the seething strife
Of auction-marts and city life.

Serenely down the busy stream
Miss Thompson floated in a dream.
Now, hovering bee-like, she would stop
Entranced before some tempting shop,
Getting in people's way and prying
At things she never thought of buying:
Now wafted on without an aim:
Until in course of time she came
To Watson's bootshop. Long she pries
At boots and shoes of every size,
Brown football-boots with bar and stud,
For boys that scuffle in the mud,
And dancing-pumps with pointed toes
Glassy as jet, and dull black bows;
Slim ladies' shoe with two-inch heel
And sprinkled beads of gold and steel—

'How anyone can wear such things!'
On either side the doorway springs
(As in a tropic jungle loom
Masses of strange thick-petalled bloom
And fruits misshapen) fold on fold
A growth of sandshoes rubber-soled,
Clambering the door-posts, branching, spawning,
Their barbarous bunches like an awning
Over the windows and the doors.
But, framed among the other stores,
Something has caught Miss Thompson's eye
(O worldliness! O vanity!)
A pair of slippers—scarlet plush.
Miss Thompson feels a conscious blush
Suffuse her face, as though her thought
Had ventured further than it ought.
But O that colour's rapturous singing
And the answer in her lone heart ringing!
She turns (O Guardian Angels stop her
From doing anything improper!),
She turns; and see, she stoops and bungles
In through the sandshoes' hanging jungles,
Away from light and common sense,
Into the shop dim-lit and dense
With smells of polish and tanned hide.

Soon from a dark recess inside,
Fat Mrs. Watson comes slip-slop
To mind the business of the shop.
She walks flat-footed with a roll—
A serviceable, homely soul,
With kindly, ugly face like dough,
Hair dull and colourless as tow.

A huge Scotch-pebble fills the space
Between her bosom and her face.
One sees her making beds all day.
Miss Thompson let her say her say
'So chilly for the time of year.
It's ages since we saw you here.'
Then, heart a-flutter, speech precise,
Describes the shoes and asks the price.
'Them, Miss? Ah, them is six-and-nine.'
Miss Thompson shudders down the spine.
(Dream of impossible romance).
She eyes them with a wistful glance,
Torn between good and evil. Yes,
For half-a-minute and no less
Miss Thompson strives with seven devils,
Then, soaring over earthly levels,
Turns from the shoes with lingering touch—
'Ah, six-and-nine is far too much.
Sorry to trouble you. Good day!'

A little farther down the way
Stands Miles's fish-shop, whence is shed
So strong a smell of fishes dead
That people of a subtler sense
Hold their breath and hurry thence.
Miss Thompson hovers there and gazes:
Her housewife's knowing eye appraises
Salt and fresh, severely cons
Kippers bright as tarnished bronze;
Great cods disposed upon the sill
Chilly and wet, with gaping gill,
Flat head, glazed eye, and mute, uncouth,
Shapeless, wan, old-woman's mouth.

Next, a row of soles and plaice
With querulous and twisted face,
And red-eyed bloaters, golden-grey;
Smoked haddocks ranked in neat array;
A group of smelts that take the light
Like slips of rainbow, pearly bright;
Silver trout with rosy spots,
And coral shrimps with keen black dots
For eyes, and hard and jointed sheath
And crisp tails curving underneath.
But there upon the sanded floor,
More wonderful in all that store
Than anything on slab or shelf,
Stood Miles, the Fishmonger, himself.
Foursquare he stood and filled the place.
His huge hands and his jolly face
Were red. He had a mouth to quaff
Pint after pint; a sounding laugh,
But wheezy at the end, and oft
His eyes bulged outward and he coughed.
Aproned he stood from chin to toe.
The apron's vertical long flow
Warped grandly outwards to display
His hale, round belly hung midway,
Whose apex was securely bound
With apron-strings wrapped round and round.

Outside, Miss Thompson, small and staid,
Felt, as she always felt, afraid
Of this huge man who laughed so loud,
And drew the notice of the crowd.
Awhile she paused in timid thought
Then promptly hurried in and bought

'Two kippers, please. Yes, lovely weather.'
'Two kippers? Sixpence altogether':
And in her basket laid the pair
Wrapped face to face in newspaper.

Then, on she went, as one half blind,
For things were stirring in her mind:
Then, turned about with fixed intent
And, heading for the bootshop, went
Straight in and bought the scarlet slippers,
And popped them in beside the kippers.

So much for that. From there she tacked,
Still flushed by this decisive act,
Westward, and came without a stop
To Mr. Wren, the chemist's shop,
And stood awhile outside to see
The tall big-bellied bottles three—
Red, blue, and emerald, richly bright
Each with its burning core of light.
The bell chimed as she pushed the door.
Spotless the oilcloth on the floor,
Limpid as water each glass case,
Each thing precisely in its place.
Rows of small drawers, black-lettered each
With curious words of foreign speech,
Rose high above the other ware.
The old strange fragrance filled the air,
A fragrance like a garden pink,
But tinged with vague medicinal stink
Of camphor, soap, new sponges, blent
With chloroform and violet-scent.

And Wren the Chemist, tall and spare
Stood gaunt behind his counter there.

Quiet and very wise he seemed,
With skull-like face, bald head that gleamed:
Through spectacles his eyes looked kind.
He wore a pencil tucked behind
His ear. And never he mistakes
The wildest signs the doctor makes
Prescribing drugs. Brown paper, string,
He will not use for anything,
But all in neat white parcels packs
And sticks them up with sealing-wax.
Miss Thompson bowed and blushed, and then
Undoubting bought of Mr. Wren,
Being free from modern scepticism,
A bottle for her rheumatism:
Also some peppermints to take
In case of wind; an oval cake
Of scented soap; a penny square
Of pungent naphthaline to scare
The moth. And after Wren had wrapped
And sealed the lot, Miss Thompson clapped
Them in beside the fish and shoes:
'Good day,' she says and off she goes.

Beelike Miss Thompson, whither next?
Outside, you pause awhile, perplext,
Your bearings lost. Then all comes back
And round she wheels, hot on the track
Of Giles the Grocer: and from there
To Emilie the Milliner,
There to be tempted by the sight
Of hats and blouses fiercely bright.
(O guard Miss Thompson, Powers that Be,
From Crudeness and Vulgarity.)

Still on from shop to shop she goes
With sharp bird's eye, inquiring nose,
Prying and peering, entering some,
Oblivious of the thought of home.
The town brimmed up with deep-blue haze,
But still she stayed to flit and gaze,
Her eyes ablur with rapturous sights,
Her small soul full of small delights,
Empty her purse, her basket filled.
The traffic in the town was stilled.
The clock struck six. Men thronged the inns.
Dear, dear, she should be home long since.

Then as she climbed the misty downs,
The lamps were lighted in the town's
Small streets. She saw them star by star
Multiplying from afar:
Till, mapped beneath her, she could trace
Each street, and the wide square market-place,
Sunk deeper and deeper as she went
Higher up the steep ascent.
And all that soul-uplifting stir
Step by step fell back from her,
The glory gone, the blossoming
Shrivelled, and she, a small, frail thing,
Carrying her laden basket. Till
Darkness and silence of the hill
Received her in their restful care
And stars came dropping through the air.

But loudly, sweetly sang the slippers
In the basket with the kippers;
And loud and sweet the answering thrills
From her lone heart on the hills.

MARTIN ARMSTRONG

21

ART thou poor, yet hast thou golden slumbers?
        O sweet content!
Art thou rich, yet is thy mind perplex'd?
        O punishment!
Dost thou laugh to see how fools are vex'd
To add to golden numbers golden numbers?
O sweet content! O sweet, O sweet content!
    Work apace, apace, apace, apace;
    Honest labour bears a lovely face;
Then hey nonny nonny—hey nonny nonny!

Canst drink the waters of the crispèd spring?
        O sweet content!
Swim'st thou in wealth, yet sink'st in thine own tears?
        O punishment!
Then he that patiently want's burden bears,
No burden bears, but is a king, a king!
O sweet content! O sweet, O sweet content!
    Work apace, apace, apace, apace;
    Honest labour bears a lovely face;
Then hey nonny nonny—hey nonny nonny!

                       T. DEKKER

8   *The Rider at the Gate*

A WINDY night was blowing on Rome,
The cressets guttered on Caesar's home,
The fish-boats, moored at the bridge, were breaking
The rush of the river to yellow foam.

The hinges whined to the shutters shaking,
When clip-clop-clep came a horse-hoof raking
The stones of the road at Caesar's gate;
The spear-butts jarred at the guard's awaking.

'Who goes there?' said the guard at the gate.
'What is the news, that you ride so late?'
'News most pressing, that must be spoken
To Caesar alone, and that cannot wait.'

'The Caesar sleeps; you must show a token
That the news suffice that he be awoken.
What is the news, and whence do you come?
For no light cause may his sleep be broken.'

'Out of the dark of the sands I come,
From the dark of death, with news for Rome.
A word so fell that it must be uttered
Though it strike the soul of the Caesar dumb.'

Caesar turned in his bed and muttered,
With a struggle for breath the lamp-flame guttered;
Calpurnia heard her husband moan:
        'The house is falling,
The beaten men come into their own.'

'Speak your word,' said the guard at the gate;
'Yes, but bear it to Caesar straight,
Say, "Your murderer's knives are honing,
Your killer's gang is lying in wait."

'Out of the wind that is blowing and moaning,
Through the city palace and the country loaning,
I cry, "For the world's sake, Caesar, beware,
And take this warning as my atoning.

' "Beware of the Court, of the palace stair,
Of the downcast friend who speaks so fair,
Keep from the Senate, for Death is going
On many men's feet to meet you there."

'I, who am dead, have ways of knowing
Of the crop of death that the quick are sowing.
I, who was Pompey, cry it aloud
From the dark of death, from the wind blowing.

'I, who was Pompey, once was proud,
Now I lie in the sand without a shroud;
I cry to Caesar out of my pain,
"Caesar, beware, your death is vowed." '

The light grew grey on the window-pane,
The windcocks swung in a burst of rain,
The window of Caesar flung unshuttered,
The horse-hoofs died into wind again.

Caesar turned in his bed and muttered,
With a struggle for breath the lamp-flame guttered;
Calpurnia heard her husband moan:
        'The house is falling,
The beaten men come into their own.'

JOHN MASEFIELD

9   *A St. Helena Lullaby*

'How far is St. Helena from a little child at play?'
What makes you want to wander there with all the world
    between?
Oh, Mother, call your son again or else he'll run away.
(*No one thinks of winter when the grass is green!*)

'How far is St. Helena from a fight in Paris Street?'
I haven't time to answer now—the men are falling fast.
The guns begin to thunder, and the drums begin to beat.
(*If you take the first step, you will take the last!*)

'How far is St. Helena from the field of Austerlitz?'
You couldn't hear me if I told—so loud the cannon roar.
But not so far for people who are living by their wits.
(*"Gay go up" means "Gay go down" the wide world o'er!*)

'How far is St. Helena from an Emperor of France?'
I cannot see—I cannot tell—the Crowns they dazzle so.
The Kings sit down to dinner, and the Queens stand up to
      dance.
(*After open weather you may look for snow!*)

'How far is St. Helena from the Capes of Trafalgar?'
A longish way—a longish way—with ten year more to run.
It's South across the water underneath a falling star.
(*What you cannot finish you must leave undone!*)

'How far is St. Helena from the Beresina ice?'
An ill way—a chill way—the ice begins to crack.
But not so far for gentlemen who never took advice.
(*When you can't go forward you must e'en come back!*)

'How far is St. Helena from the field of Waterloo?'
A near way—a clear way—the ship will take you soon.
A pleasant place for gentlemen with little left to do.
(*Morning never tries you till the afternoon!*)

'How far from St. Helena to the Gate of Heaven's Grace?'
That no one knows—that no one knows—and no one ever
      will.
But fold your hands across your heart and cover up your face,
And after all your trapesings, child, lie still!

RUDYARD KIPLING

How happy is he born and taught
　That serveth not another's will;
Whose armour is his honest thought,
　And simple truth his utmost skill!

Whose passions not his masters are;
　Whose soul is still prepared for death,
Untied unto the world by care
　Of public fame or private breath;

Who envies none that chance doth raise,
　Nor vice; who never understood
How deepest wounds are given by praise;
　Nor rules of state, but rules of good;

Who hath his life from rumours freed;
　Whose conscience is his strong retreat;
Whose state can neither flatterers feed,
　Nor ruin make oppressors great;

Who God doth late and early pray
　More of His grace than gifts to lend;
And entertains the harmless day
　With a religious book or friend;

This man is freed from servile bands
　Of hope to rise or fear to fall:
Lord of himself, though not of lands,
　And having nothing, yet hath all.

SIR HENRY WOTTON

11 *There was an Indian*

THERE was an Indian, who had known no change,
  Who strayed content along a sunlit beach
Gathering shells. He heard a sudden strange
  Commingled noise: looked up; and gasped for speech.

For in the bay, where nothing was before,
  Moved on the sea, by magic, huge canoes,
With bellying cloths on poles, and not one oar,
  And fluttering coloured signs and clambering crews.

And he, in fear, this naked man alone,
  His fallen hands forgetting all their shells,
His lips gone pale, knelt low behind a stone,
  And stared, and saw, and did not understand,
Columbus's doom-burdened caravels
  Slant to the shore, and all their seamen land.

J. C. SQUIRE

12 *Simon Legree*

LEGREE's big house was white and green.
His cotton-fields were the best to be seen.
He had strong horses and opulent cattle,
And bloodhounds bold, with chains that would rattle.
His garret was full of curious things:
Books of magic, bags of gold,
And rabbits' feet on long twine strings.
But he went down to the Devil.

Legree, he sported a brass-buttoned coat,
A snake-skin necktie, a blood-red shirt.
Legree, he had a beard like a goat,
And a thick hairy neck, and eyes like dirt.
His puffed-out cheeks were fish-belly white,
He had great long teeth, and an appetite.
He ate raw meat, 'most every meal,
And rolled his eyes till the cat would squeal.
His fist was an enormous size
To mash poor niggers that told him lies:
He was surely a witch-man in disguise.
But he went down to the Devil.

He wore hip-boots, and would wade all day
To capture his slaves that had fled away.
But he went down to the Devil.
He beat poor Uncle Tom to death
Who prayed for Legree with his last breath.
Then Uncle Tom to Eva flew,
To the high sanctoriums bright and new;
And Simon Legree stared up beneath,
And cracked his heels, and ground his teeth:
And went down to the Devil.

He crossed the yard in the storm and gloom;
He went into his grand front room.
He said, 'I killed him, and I don't care.'
He kicked a hound, he gave a swear;
He tightened his belt, he took a lamp,
Went down cellar to the webs and damp.
There in the middle of the mouldy floor
He heaved up a slab; he found a door—
And went down to the Devil.

His lamp blew out, but his eyes burned bright.
Simon Legree stepped down all night—
Down, down to the Devil.
Simon Legree he reached the place,
He saw one half of the human race,
He saw the Devil on a wide green throne,
Gnawing the meat from a big ham-bone,
And he said to Mister Devil:

'I see that you have much to eat—
A red ham-bone is surely sweet.
I see that you have lion's feet;
I see your frame is fat and fine,
I see you drink your poison wine—
Blood and burning turpentine.'

And the Devil said to Simon Legree:
'I like your style, so wicked and free.
Come sit and share my throne with me.
And let us bark and revel.'
And there they sit and gnash their teeth,
And each one wears a hop-vine wreath.
They are matching pennies and shooting craps,
They are playing poker and taking naps.
And old Legree is fat and fine:
He eats the fire, he drinks the wine—
Blood and burning turpentine—
Down, down with the Devil;
Down, down with the Devil;
Down, down with the Devil.

VACHEL LINDSAY

THIS ae nighte, this ae nighte,
  Every nighte and alle,
Fire and fleet and candle-lighte,
  And Christe receive thy saule.

When thou from hence away art past,
  Every nighte and alle,
To Whinny-muir thou com'st at last;
  And Christe receive thy saule.

If ever thou gavest hosen and shoon,
  Every nighte and alle,
Sit thee down and put them on;
  And Christe receive thy saule.

If hosen and shoon thou ne'er gav'st nane,
  Every nighte and alle,
The whinnes sall prick thee to the bare bane;
  And Christe receive thy saule.

From Whinny-muir when thou may'st pass,
  Every nighte and alle,
To Brig o' Dread thou com'st at last;
  And Christe receive thy saule.

From Brig o' Dread when thou may'st pass,
  Every nighte and alle,
To Purgatory fire thou com'st at last;
  And Christe receive thy saule.

fleet, house-room.   *Whinny*, gorse.   *Brig*, bridge.

If ever thou gavest meat or drink,
   Every nighte and alle,
The fire sall never make thee shrink,
   And Christe receive thy saule.

If meat and drink thou ne'er gav'st nane,
   Every nighte and alle,
The fire will burn thee to the bare bane;
   And Christe receive thy saule.

This ae nighte, this ae nighte,
   Every nighte and alle,
Fire and fleet and candle-lighte;
   And Christe receive thy saule.

BALLAD

14   *The Wife of Usher's Well*

THERE lived a wife at Usher's well,
   And a wealthy wife was she;
She had three stout and stalwart sons,
   And sent them o'er the sea.

They hadna been a week from her,
   A week but barely ane,
When word came to the carline wife
   That her three sons were gane.

They hadna been a week from her,
   A week but barely three,
When word came to the carline wife
   That her sons she'd never see.

     carline, old woman.

'I wish the wind may never cease,
    Nor fashes in the flood,
Till my three sons come hame to me,
    In earthly flesh and blood!'

It fell about the Martinmas,
    When nights are lang and mirk,
The carline wife's three sons came hame,
    And their hats were o' the birk.

It neither grew in syke nor ditch,
    Nor yet in ony sheugh;
But at the gates o' Paradise
    That birk grew fair eneugh.

'Blow up the fire, my maidens!
    Bring water from the well!
For a' my house shall feast this night,
    Since my three sons are well.'

And she has made to them a bed,
    She's made it large and wide;
And she's ta'en her mantle her about,
    Sat down at the bedside.

Up then crew the red, red cock,
    And up and crew the grey;
The eldest to the youngest said,
    ''Tis time we were away.'

The cock he hadna craw'd but once,
    And clapp'd his wings at a',
When the youngest to the eldest said,
    'Brother, we must awa.

fashes, troubles.   *birk*, birch.   *syke*, marsh.   *sheugh*, trench.

32

'The cock doth craw, the day doth daw,
    The channerin' worm doth chide;
Gin we be miss'd out o' our place,
    A sair pain we maun bide.'

'Lie still, lie still but a little wee while,
    Lie still but if we may;
Gin my mother should miss us when she wakes,
    She'll go mad ere it be day.'

'Fare ye weel, my mother dear!
    Farewell to barn and byre!
And fare ye weel, the bonny lass
    That kindles my mother's fire!'

BALLAD

channering, fretting.

Sister Helen

'WHY did you melt your waxen man,
        Sister Helen?
To-day is the third since you began.'
'The time was long, yet the time ran,
        Little brother.'
    (*O Mother, Mary Mother,*
Three days to-day, between Hell and Heaven!)

'But if you have done your work aright,
        Sister Helen,
You'll let me play, for you said I might.'
'Be very still in your play to-night,
        Little brother.'
    (*O Mother, Mary Mother,*
Third night, to-night, between Hell and Heaven!)

'You said it must melt ere vesper-bell,
              Sister Helen;
If now it be molten, all is well.'
'Even so,—nay, peace! you cannot tell,
              Little brother.'
        (*O Mother, Mary Mother,*
O what is this, between Hell and Heaven?)

'Oh the waxen knave was plump to-day,
              Sister Helen;
How like dead folk he has dropped away!'
'Nay now, of the dead what can you say,
              Little brother?'
        (*O Mother, Mary Mother,*
What of the dead, between Hell and Heaven?)

'See, see, the sunken pile of wood,
              Sister Helen,
Shines through the thinned wax red as blood!'
'Nay now, when looked you yet on blood,
              Little brother?'
        (*O Mother, Mary Mother,*
How pale she is, between Hell and Heaven!)

'Now close your eyes, for they're sick and sore,
              Sister Helen,
And I'll play without the gallery door.'
'Aye, let me rest,—I'll lie on the floor,
              Little brother.'
        (*O Mother, Mary Mother,*
What rest to-night, between Hell and Heaven?)

'Here high up on the balcony,
                Sister Helen,
The moon flies face to face with me.'
'Aye, look and say whatever you see,
                Little brother.'
            (*O Mother, Mary Mother,*
What sight to-night, between Hell and Heaven?)

'Outside it's merry in the wind's wake,
                Sister Helen;
In the shaken trees the chill stars shake.'
'Hush, heard you a horse-tread as you spake,
                Little brother?'
            (*O Mother, Mary Mother,*
What sound to-night, between Hell and Heaven?)

'I hear a horse-tread, and I see,
                Sister Helen,
Three horsemen that ride terribly.'
'Little brother, whence come the three,
                Little brother?'
            (*O Mother, Mary Mother,*
Whence should they come, between Hell and Heaven?)

'They come by the hill-verge from Boyne Bar,
                Sister Helen,
And one draws nigh, but two are afar.'
'Look, look, do you know them who they are,
                Little brother?'
            (*O Mother, Mary Mother,*
Who should they be, between Hell and Heaven?)

'Oh, it's Keith of Eastholm rides so fast,
      Sister Helen,
For I know the white mane on the blast.'
'The hour has come, has come at last,
      Little brother!'
      (O Mother, Mary Mother,
Her hour at last, between Hell and Heaven!)

'He has made a sign and called Halloo!
      Sister Helen,
And he says that he would speak with you.'
'Oh tell him I fear the frozen dew,
      Little brother.'
      (O Mother, Mary Mother,
Why laughs she thus, between Hell and Heaven?)

'The wind is loud, but I hear him cry,
      Sister Helen,
That Keith of Ewern's like to die.'
'And he and thou, and thou and I,
      Little brother.'
      (O Mother, Mary Mother,
And they and we, between Hell and Heaven!)

'Three days ago, on his marriage-morn,
      Sister Helen,
He sickened, and lies since then forlorn.'
'For bridegroom's side is the bride a thorn,
      Little brother?'
      (O Mother, Mary Mother,
Cold bridal cheer, between Hell and Heaven!)

'Three days and nights he has lain abed,
        Sister Helen,
And he prays in torment to be dead.'
'The thing may chance, if he have prayed,
        Little brother!'
    (O Mother, Mary Mother,
If he have prayed, between Hell and Heaven!)

'But he has not ceased to cry to-day,
        Sister Helen,
That you should take your curse away.'
'*My* prayer was heard,—he need but pray,
        Little brother!'
    (O Mother, Mary Mother,
Shall God not hear, between Hell and Heaven?)

'But he says, till you take back your ban,
        Sister Helen,
His soul would pass, yet never can.'
'Nay then, shall I slay a living man,
        Little brother?'
    (O Mother, Mary Mother,
A living soul, between Hell and Heaven!)

'But he calls for ever on your name,
        Sister Helen,
And says that he melts before a flame.'
'My heart for his pleasure fared the same,
        Little brother.'
    (O Mother, Mary Mother,
Fire at the heart, between Hell and Heaven!)

'Here's Keith of Westholm riding fast,
          Sister Helen,
For I know the white plume on the blast.'
'The hour, the sweet hour I forecast,
          Little brother!'
          (*O Mother, Mary Mother,*
Is the hour sweet, between Hell and Heaven?)

'He stops to speak, and he stills his horse,
          Sister Helen;
But his words are drowned in the wind's course.'
'Nay hear, nay hear, you must hear perforce,
          Little brother!'
          (*O Mother, Mary Mother,*
What word now heard, between Hell and Heaven?)

'Oh he says that Keith of Ewern's cry,
          Sister Helen,
Is ever to see you ere he die.'
'In all that his soul sees, there am I,
          Little brother!'
          (*O Mother, Mary Mother,*
The soul's one sight, between Hell and Heaven!)

'He sends a ring and a broken coin,
          Sister Helen,
And bids you mind the banks of Boyne.'
'What else he broke will he ever join,
          Little brother?'
          (*O Mother, Mary Mother,*
No, never joined, between Hell and Heaven!)

'He yields you these and craves full fain,
         Sister Helen,
You pardon him in his mortal pain.'
'What else he took will he give again,
         Little brother?'
      (O Mother, Mary Mother,
Not twice to give, between Hell and Heaven!)

'He calls your name in an agony,
         Sister Helen,
That even dead Love must weep to see.'
'Hate, born of Love, is blind as he,
         Little brother!'
      (O Mother, Mary Mother,
Love turned to hate, between Hell and Heaven!)

'Oh it's Keith of Keith now that rides fast,
         Sister Helen,
For I know the white hair on the blast.'
'The short, short hour will soon be past,
         Little brother!'
      (O Mother, Mary Mother,
Will soon be past, between Hell and Heaven!)

'He looks at me and he tries to speak,
         Sister Helen,
But oh! his voice is sad and weak!'
'What here should the mighty Baron seek,
         Little brother?'
      (O Mother, Mary Mother,
Is this the end, between Hell and Heaven?)

'Oh his son still cries, if you forgive,
        Sister Helen,
The body dies, but the soul shall live.'
'Fire shall forgive me as I forgive,
        Little brother!'
        (O Mother, Mary Mother,
As she forgives, between Hell and Heaven!)

'Oh he prays you, as his heart would rive,
        Sister Helen,
To save his dear son's soul alive.'
'Fire cannot slay it, it shall thrive,
        Little brother!'
        (O Mother, Mary Mother,
Alas, alas, between Hell and Heaven!)

'He cries to you, kneeling in the road,
        Sister Helen,
To go with him for the love of God!'
'The way is long to his son's abode,
        Little brother.'
        (O Mother, Mary Mother,
The way is long, between Hell and Heaven!)

'A lady's here, by a dark steed brought,
        Sister Helen,
So darkly clad, I saw her not.'
'See her now or never see aught,
        Little brother!'
        (O Mother, Mary Mother,
What more to see, between Hell and Heaven?)

'Her hood falls back, and the moon shines fair,
          Sister Helen,
On the Lady of Ewern's golden hair.'
'Blest hour of my power and her despair,
          Little brother!'
          (*O Mother, Mary Mother,*
Hour blest and bann'd, between Hell and Heaven!)

'Pale, pale her cheeks, that in pride did glow,
          Sister Helen,
'Neath the bridal-wreath three days ago.'
'One morn for pride and three days for woe,
          Little brother!'
          (*O Mother, Mary Mother,*
Three days, three nights, between Hell and Heaven!)

'Her clasped hands stretch from her bending head,
          Sister Helen;
With the loud wind's wail her sobs are wed.'
'What wedding-strains hath her bridal-bed,
          Little brother?'
          (*O Mother, Mary Mother,*
What strain but death's, between Hell and Heaven?)

'She may not speak, she sinks in a swoon,
          Sister Helen,—
She lifts her lips and gasps on the moon.'
'Oh! might I but hear her soul's blithe tune,
          Little brother!'
          (*O Mother, Mary Mother,*
Her woe's dumb cry, between Hell and Heaven!)

'They've caught her to Westholm's saddle-bow,
              Sister Helen,
And her moonlit hair gleams white in its flow!'
'Let it turn whiter than winter snow,
              Little brother!'
          (*O Mother, Mary Mother,*
  Woe-withered gold, between Hell and Heaven!)

'O Sister Helen, you heard the bell,
              Sister Helen!
More loud than the vesper-chime it fell.'
'No vesper-chime, but a dying knell,
              Little brother!'
          (*O Mother, Mary Mother,*
  His dying knell, between Hell and Heaven!)

'Alas! but I fear the heavy sound,
              Sister Helen;
Is it in the sky or in the ground?'
'Say, have they turned their horses round,
              Little brother?'
          (*O Mother, Mary Mother,*
  What would she more, between Hell and Heaven?)

'They have raised the old man from his knee,
              Sister Helen,
And they ride in silence hastily.'
'More fast the naked soul doth flee,
              Little brother!'
          (*O Mother, Mary Mother,*
  The naked soul, between Hell and Heaven!)

'Flank to flank are the three steeds gone,
            Sister Helen,
But the lady's dark steed goes alone.'
'And lonely her bridegroom's soul hath flown,
            Little brother.'
            (*O Mother, Mary Mother,*
The lonely ghost, between Hell and Heaven!)

'Oh the wind is sad in the iron chill,
            Sister Helen,
And weary sad they look by the hill.'
'But he and I are sadder still,
            Little brother!'
            (*O Mother, Mary Mother,*
Most sad of all, between Hell and Heaven!)

'See, see the wax has dropped from its place,
            Sister Helen,
And the flames are winning up apace!'
'Yet here they burn but for a space,
            Little brother!'
            (*O Mother, Mary Mother,*
Here for a space, between Hell and Heaven!)

'Ah! what white thing at the door has cross'd?
            Sister Helen?
Ah! what is this that sighs in the frost?'
'A soul that's lost as mine is lost,
            Little brother!'
            (*O Mother, Mary Mother,*
Lost, lost, all lost, between Hell and Heaven!)

D. G. ROSSETTI

BEN BATTLE was a soldier bold,
   And used to war's alarms:
But a cannon-ball took off his legs,
   So he laid down his arms!

Now as they bore him off the field,
   Said he, 'Let others shoot,
For here I leave my second leg,
   And the Forty-second Foot!'

The army-surgeons made him limbs:
   Said he,—'They're only pegs:
But there's as wooden members quite
   As represent my legs!'

Now Ben he loved a pretty maid,
   Her name was Nelly Gray;
So he went to pay her his devours
   When he'd devoured his pay!

But when he called on Nelly Gray,
   She made him quite a scoff;
And when she saw his wooden legs,
   Began to take them off!

'O, Nelly Gray! O, Nelly Gray!
   Is this your love so warm?
The love that loves a scarlet coat
   Should be more uniform!'

Said she, 'I loved a soldier once,
  For he was blythe and brave;
But I will never have a man
  With both legs in the grave!

'Before you had those timber toes,
  Your love I did allow,
But then, you know, you stand upon
  Another footing now!'

'O, Nelly Gray! O, Nelly Gray!
  For all your jeering speeches,
At duty's call, I left my legs
  In Badajos's *breaches!*'

'Why, then,' said she, 'you've lost the feet
  Of legs in war's alarms,
And now you cannot wear your shoes
  Upon your feats of arms!'

'O, false and fickle Nelly Gray;
  I know why you refuse:—
Though I've no feet—some other man
  Is standing in my shoes!

'I wish I ne'er had seen your face;
  But, now, a long farewell!
For you will be my death;—alas!
  You will not be my *Nell!*'

Now when he went from Nelly Gray,
  His heart so heavy got—
And life was such a burthen grown,
  It made him take a knot!

So round his melancholy neck,
   A rope he did entwine,
And, for his second time in life,
   Enlisted in the Line!

One end he tied around a beam,
   And then removed his pegs,
And, as his legs were off,—of course,
   He soon was off his legs!

And there he hung, till he was dead
   As any nail in town,—
For though distress had cut him up,
   It could not cut him down!

A dozen men sat on his corpse,
   To find out why he died—
And they buried Ben in four crossroads,
   With a *stake* in his inside!

T. HOOD

17   *O Mistress Mine*

O MISTRESS mine, where are you roaming?
O, stay and hear; your true-love's coming,
   That can sing both high and low:
Trip no further, pretty sweeting;
Journeys end in lovers' meeting,
   Every wise man's son doth know.

What is love? 'tis not hereafter;
Present mirth hath present laughter;
   What's to come is still unsure:
In delay there lies no plenty;
Then come kiss me, sweet-and-twenty,
   Youth's a stuff will not endure.

W. SHAKESPEARE

18   *The Shandon Bells*

WITH deep affection
And recollection,
I often think of
   Those Shandon bells,
Whose sounds so wild would,
In the days of childhood,
Fling round my cradle
   Their magic spells.
On this I ponder
Where'er I wander,
And thus grow fonder,
   Sweet Cork, of thee;
With thy bells of Shandon,
That sound so grand on
The pleasant waters
   Of the River Lee.
I've heard bells chiming
Full many a clime in,
Tolling sublime in
   Cathedral shrine,
While at a glibe rate
Brass tongues would vibrate—

But all their music
   Spoke naught like thine;
For memory, dwelling
On each proud swelling
Of thy belfrey knelling
   Its bold notes free,
Made the bells of Shandon
Sound far more grand on
The pleasant waters
   Of the River Lee.
I've heard bells tolling
Old Adrian's Mole in,
Their thunder rolling
   From the Vatican,
And cymbals glorious
Swinging uproarious
In the gorgeous turrets
   Of Notre Dame;
But thy sounds were sweeter
Than the dome of Peter
Flings o'er the Tiber,
   Pealing solemnly;—
O! the bells of Shandon
Sound far more grand on
The pleasant waters
   Of the River Lee.
There's a bell in Moscow,
While on tower and kiosk O
In Saint Sophia
   The Turkman gets;
And loud in air
Calls men to prayer
From the tapering summit
   Of tall minarets.

Such empty phantom
I freely grant them;
But there is an anthem
   More dear to me,—
'Tis the bells of Shandon
That sound so grand on
The pleasant waters
   Of the River Lee.

F. S. MAHONY

19   *The Bugle*

THE splendour falls on castle walls
   And snowy summits old in story:
The long light shakes across the lakes,
   And the wild cataract leaps in glory.
Blow, bugle, blow, set the wild echoes flying,
Blow, bugle; answer, echoes, dying, dying, dying.

O hark, O hear! how thin and clear,
   And thinner, clearer, farther going!
O sweet and far from cliff and scar
   The horns of Elfland faintly blowing!
Blow, let us hear the purple glens replying:
Blow, bugle; answer, echoes, dying, dying, dying.

O love, they die in yon rich sky,
   They faint on hill or field or river:
Our echoes roll from soul to soul,
   And grow for ever and for ever.
Blow, bugle, blow, set the wild echoes flying,
And answer, echoes, answer, dying, dying, dying.

LORD TENNYSON

I COME from haunts of coot and hern,
 I make a sudden sally
And sparkle out among the fern,
 To bicker down a valley.

By thirty hills I hurry down,
 Or slip between the ridges,
By twenty thorps, a little town,
 And half a hundred bridges.

Till last by Philip's farm I flow
 To join the brimming river,
For men may come and men may go,
 But I go on for ever.

I chatter over stony ways,
 In little sharps and trebles,
I bubble into eddying bays,
 I babble on the pebbles.

With many a curve my banks I fret
 By many a field and fallow,
And many a fairy foreland set
 With willow-weed and mallow.

I chatter, chatter, as I flow
 To join the brimming river,
For men may come and men may go,
 But I go on for ever.

50

I wind about, and in and out,
    With here a blossom sailing,
And here and there a lusty trout,
    And here and there a grayling.

And here and there a foamy flake
    Upon me, as I travel
With many a silvery waterbreak
    Above the golden gravel,

And draw them all along, and flow
    To join the brimming river,
For men may come and men may go,
    But I go on for ever.

I steal by lawns and grassy plots,
    I slide by hazel covers;
I move the sweet forget-me-nots
    That grow for happy lovers.

I slip, I slide, I gloom, I glance,
    Among my skimming swallows;
I make the netted sunbeam dance
    Against my sandy shallows.

I murmur under moon and stars,
    In brambly wildernesses;
I linger by my shingly bars;
    I loiter round my cresses;

And out again I curve and flow
    To join the brimming river,
For men may come and men may go,
    But I go on for ever.

LORD TENNYSON

BREAK, break, break,
 On thy cold grey stones, O Sea!
And I would that my tongue could utter
 The thoughts that arise in me.

O well for the fisherman's boy,
 That he shouts with his sister at play!
O well for the sailor lad,
 That he sings in his boat on the bay!

And the stately ships go on
 To their haven under the hill;
But O for the touch of a vanish'd hand,
 And the sound of a voice that is still!

Break, break, break,
 At the foot of thy crags, O Sea!
But the tender grace of a day that is dead
 Will never come back to me.

LORD TENNYSON

'O MARY, go and call the cattle home,
 And call the cattle home,
 And call the cattle home
 Across the sands of Dee;'
The western wind was wild and dank with foam,
 And all alone went she.

The western tide crept up along the sand,
    And o'er and o'er the sand,
    And round and round the sand,
  As far as eye could see.
The rolling mist came down and hid the land:
  And never home came she.

'Oh, is it weed, or fish, or floating hair—
    A tress of golden hair,
    A drownèd maiden's hair
  Above the nets at sea?
Was never salmon yet that shone so fair
  Among the stakes on Dee.'

They rowed her in across the rolling foam,
    The cruel, crawling foam,
    The cruel, hungry foam,
  To her grave beside the sea:
But still the boatmen hear her call the cattle home,
  Across the sands of Dee.

CHARLES KINGSLEY

23   *To the Virgins, to make much of Time*

GATHER ye rosebuds while ye may,
    Old Time is still a-flying:
And this same flower that smiles to-day
    To-morrow will be dying.

The glorious lamp of heaven, the sun,
    The higher he's a-getting,
The sooner will his race be run,
    And nearer he's to setting.

53

That age is best which is the first,
   When youth and blood are warmer;
But being spent, the worse, and worst
   Times still succeed the former.

Then be not coy, but use your time,
   And while ye may, go marry:
For having lost but once your prime,
   You may for ever tarry.

R. HERRICK

24   *The Joy of Living*

(From *Saul*)

OH, the wild joys of living! the leaping from rock up to
   rock,
The strong rending of boughs from the fir-tree, the cool
   silver shock
Of the plunge in a pool's living water, the hunt of the bear,
And the sultriness showing the lion is couched in his lair.
And the meal, the rich dates yellowed over with gold dust
   divine,
And the locust-flesh steeped in the pitcher, the full draught
   of wine,
And the sleep in the dried river-channel where bullrushes
   tell
That the water was wont to go warbling so softly and well.
How good is man's life, the mere living! how fit to employ
All the heart and the soul and the senses for ever in joy!

ROBERT BROWNING

25

Home Thoughts from Abroad

OH, to be in England
Now that April's there,
And whoever wakes in England
Sees, some morning, unaware,
That the lowest boughs and the brushwood sheaf
Round the elm-tree bole are in tiny leaf,
While the chaffinch sings on the orchard bough
In England—now!
And after April, when May follows,
And the whitethroat builds, and all the swallows!
Hark, where my blossomed pear-tree in the hedge
Leans to the field and scatters on the clover
Blossoms and dewdrops—at the bent spray's edge—
That's the wise thrush; he sings each song twice over,
Lest you should think he never could recapture
The first fine careless rapture!
And though the fields look rough with hoary dew,
All will be gay when noontide wakes anew
The buttercups, the little children's dower
—Far brighter than this gaudy melon-flower.

ROBERT BROWNING

Home-thoughts, from the Sea

NOBLY, nobly Cape Saint Vincent to the North-West died
away;
Sunset ran, one glorious blood-red, reeking into Cadiz Bay;
Bluish mid the burning water, full in face Trafalgar lay;
In the dimmest North-East distance, dawned Gibraltar grand
and grey;

'Here and here did England help me: how can I help Eng-
    land?'—say,
Whoso turns as I, this evening, turn to God to praise and
    pray,
While Jove's planet rises yonder, silent over Africa.

ROBERT BROWNING

27   *This Royal Throne of Kings*

THIS royal throne of kings, this scept'red isle,
This earth of majesty, this seat of Mars,
This other Eden, demi-Paradise;
This fortress, built by nature for herself
Against infection and the hand of war;
This happy breed of men, this little world;
This precious stone set in a silver sea,
Which serves it in the office of a wall,
Or as a moat defensive to a house,
Against the envy of less happier lands;
This blessed plot, this earth, this realm, this England,
This nurse, this teeming womb of royal kings,
Fear'd by their breed, and famous by their birth,
Renowned for their deeds as far from home—
For Christian service and true chivalry,—
As is the sepulchre, in stubborn Jewry,
Of the world's ransom, blessèd Mary's son;
This land of such dear souls, this dear dear land,
Dear for her reputation through the world,
Is now leas'd out, I die pronouncing it,
Like to a tenement or pelting farm:
England, bound in with the triumphant sea,
Whose rocky shore beats back the envious siege
Of watery Neptune, is now bound in with shame,

With inky blots, and rotten parchment bonds:
That England, that was wont to conquer others,
Hath made a shameful conquest of itself.
Ah, would the scandal vanish with my life,
How happy then were my ensuing death!

W. SHAKESPEARE

28   *A Ballad to Queen Elizabeth*

KING PHILIP had vaunted his claims;
  He had sworn for a year he would sack us;
With an army of heathenish names
  He was coming to fagot and stack us;
  Like the thieves of the sea he would track us,
And shatter our ships on the main;
  But we had bold Neptune to back us,—
And where are the galleons of Spain?

His carackes were christened of dames
  To the kirtles whereof he would tack us;
With his saints and his gilded stern-frames,
  He had thought like an egg-shell to crack us:
  Now Howard may get to his Flaccus,
And Drake to his Devon again,
  And Hawkins bowl rubbers to Bacchus,—
For where are the galleons of Spain?

Let his Majesty hang to St. James
  The axe that he whetted to hack us;
He must play at some lustier games
  Or at sea he can hope to out-thwack us;

To his mines of Peru he would pack us
To tug at his bullet and chain;
   Alas! that his Greatness should lack us!—
But where are the galleons of Spain?

Gloriana! the Don may attack us
Whenever his stomach be fain;
   He must reach us before he can rack us,
And where are the galleons of Spain?

AUSTIN DOBSON

29   *The Armada*

ATTEND, all ye who list to hear our noble England's praise;
I tell of the thrice-famous deeds she wrought in ancient days,
When that great fleet invincible against her bore in vain
The richest spoils of Mexico, the stoutest hearts of Spain.

It was about the lovely close of a warm summer day,
There came a gallant merchant-ship full sail to Plymouth
    Bay;
Her crew had seen Castile's black fleet, beyond Aurigny's
    Isle,
At earliest twilight, on the waves lie heaving many a mile.
At sunrise she escaped their van, by God's especial grace:
And the tall Pinta, till the noon, had held her close in chase.
Forthwith a guard at every gun was placed along the wall;
The beacon blazed upon the roof of Edgecumbe's lofty hall;
Many a light fishing bark put out to pry along the coast,
And with loose rein and bloody spur rode inland many a post.

With his white hair unbonneted, the stout old sheriff
    comes;
Behind him march the halberdiers; before him sound the
    drums;
His yeomen round the market cross make clear an ample
    space;
For there behoves him to set up the standard of Her Grace.
And haughtily the trumpets peal and gaily dance the bells,
As slow upon the labouring wind the royal blazon swells.
Look how the Lion of the sea lifts up his ancient crown,
And underneath his deadly paw treads the gay lilies down.
So stalked he when he turned to flight, on that famed Picard
    field,
Bohemia's plume, and Genoa's bow, and Caesar's eagle
    shield.
So glared he when at Agincourt in wrath he turned to bay,
And crushed and torn beneath his claws the princely
    hunters lay.
Ho! strike the flagstaff deep, Sir Knight: ho! scatter flowers,
    fair maids:
Ho! gunners, fire a loud salute: ho! gallants, draw your blades:
Thou sun, shine on her joyously; ye breezes, waft her wide;
Our glorious SEMPER EADEM, the banner of our pride.
The freshening breeze of eve unfurled that banner's massy
    fold;
The parting gleam of sunshine kissed that haughty scroll of
    gold;
Night sank upon the dusky beach, and on the purple sea,
Such night in England ne'er had been, nor e'er again shall be.
From Eddystone to Berwick bounds, from Lynn to Milford
    Bay,
That time of slumber was as bright and busy as the day;
For swift to east and swift to west the ghastly war-flame
    spread,

High on St Michael's Mount it shone; it shone on Beachy
    Head.
Far o'er the deep the Spaniards saw, along each southern
    shire,
Cape beyond cape, in endless range, those twinkling points
    of fire.
The fisher left his skiff to rock on Tamar's glittering waves:
The rugged miners poured to war from Mendip's sunless
    caves:
O'er Longleat's towers, o'er Cranbourne's oaks, the fiery
    herald flew:
He roused the shepherds of Stonehenge, the rangers of
    Beaulieu.
Right sharp and quick the bells all night rang out from
    Bristol town,
And ere the day three hundred horse had met on Clifton
    Down;
The sentinel on Whitehall gate looked forth into the night,
And saw o'erhanging Richmond Hill the streak of blood-
    red light;
Then bugle's note and cannon's roar the death-like silence
    broke,
And with one start and with one cry, the royal city woke.
At once on all her stately gates arose the answering fires;
At once the wild alarum clashed from all her reeling spires;
From all the batteries of the Tower pealed loud the voice of
    fear;
And all the thousand masts of Thames sent back a louder
    cheer;
And from the furthest wards was heard the rush of hurrying
    feet,
And the broad streams of pikes and flags rushed down each
    roaring street;
And broader still became the blaze, and louder still the din,

As fast from every village round the horse came spurring in:
And eastward straight from wild Blackheath the warlike
errand went,
And roused in many an ancient hall the gallant squires of
Kent.
Southward from Surrey's pleasant hills flew those bright
couriers forth;
High on bleak Hampstead's swarthy moor they started for
the north;
And on, and on, without a pause, untired they bounded still;
All night from tower to tower they sprang: they sprang from
hill to hill:
Till the proud Peak unfurled the flag o'er Darwin's rocky
dales,
Till like volcanoes flared to heaven the stormy hills of Wales,
Till twelve fair counties saw the blaze on Malvern's lonely
height,
Till streamed in crimson on the wind the Wrekin's crest of
light,
Till broad and fierce the star came forth on Ely's stately fane,
And tower and hamlet rose in arms o'er all the boundless
plain;
Till Belvoir's lordly terraces the sign to Lincoln sent,
And Lincoln sped the message on o'er the wide vale of
Trent;
Till Skiddaw saw the fire that burned on Gaunt's em-
battled pile,
And the red glare on Skiddaw roused the burghers of
Carlisle.

LORD MACAULAY

DRAKE he's in his hammock an' a thousand mile away,
  (Capten, art tha sleepin' there below?),
Slung atween the round shot in Nombre Dios Bay,
  An' dreamin' arl the time o' Plymouth Hoe.
Yarnder lumes the Island, yarnder lie the ships,
  Wi' sailor-lads a-dancin' heel-an'-toe,
An' the shore-lights flashin', and the night-tide dashin',
  He sees et arl so plainly as he saw et long ago.

Drake he was a Devon man, an' rüled the Devon seas,
  (Capten, art tha sleepin' there below?),
Rovin' tho' his death fell, he went wi' heart at ease,
  An' dreamin' arl the time o' Plymouth Hoe.
'Take my drum to England, hang et by the shore,
  Strike et when your powder's runnin' low;
If the Dons sight Devon, I'll quit the port o' Heaven,
  An' drum them up the channel as we drummed them long
    ago.'

Drake he's in his hammock till the great Armadas come,
  (Capten, art tha sleepin' there below?),
Slung atween the round shot, listenin' for the drum,
  An' dreamin' arl the time o' Plymouth Hoe.
Call him on the deep sea, call him up the Sound,
  Call him when ye sail to meet the foe;
Where the old trade's plyin' an' the old flag flyin'
  They shall find him ware an' wakin', as they found him
    long ago!

SIR HENRY NEWBOLT

HE gave us all a good-bye cheerily
   At the first dawn of day;
We dropped him down the side full drearily
   When the light died away.
It's a dead dark watch that he's a-keeping there,
And a long, long night that lags a-creeping there,
Where the Trades and the tides roll over him
   And the great ships go by.

He's there alone with green seas rocking him
   For a thousand miles round;
He's there alone with dumb things mocking him,
   And we're homeward bound.
It's a long, lone watch that he's a-keeping there,
And a dead cold night that lags a-creeping there,
While the months and the years roll over him
   And the great ships go by.

I wonder if the tramps come near enough
   As they thrash to and fro,
And the battle-ships' bells ring clear enough
   To be heard down below;
If through all the lone watch that he's a-keeping there,
And the long, cold night that lags a-creeping there,
The voices of the sailor-men shall comfort him
   When the great ships go by.

SIR HENRY NEWBOLT

THE blue laguna rocks and quivers,
  Dull gurgling eddies twist and spin,
The climate does for people's livers,
  It's a nasty place to anchor in
    Is Spanish port,
    Fever port,
    Port of Holy Peter.

The town begins on the sea-beaches,
  And the town's mad with the stinging flies,
The drinking water's mostly leeches,
  It's a far remove from Paradise
    Is Spanish port,
    Fever port,
    Port of Holy Peter.

There's sand-bagging and throat-slitting,
  And quiet graves in the sea slime,
Stabbing, of course, and rum-hitting,
  Dirt, and drink, and stink, and crime,
    In Spanish port,
    Fever port,
    Port of Holy Peter.

All the day the wind's blowing
  From the sick swamp below the hills,
All the night the plague's growing,
  And the dawn brings the fever chills,
    In Spanish port,
    Fever port,
    Port of Holy Peter.

You get a thirst there's no slaking,
  You get the chills and fever-shakes,
Tongue yellow and head aching,
  And then the sleep that never wakes.
And all the year the heat's baking,
  The sea rots and the earth quakes,
    In Spanish port,
    Fever port,
    Port of Holy Peter.

JOHN MASEFIELD

33   *Flannan Isle*

THOUGH three men dwell on Flannan Isle
To keep the lamp alight,
As we steer'd under the lee we caught
No glimmer through the night!

A passing ship at dawn had brought
The news, and quickly we set sail
To find out what strange thing might ail
The keepers of the deep-sea light.

The winter day broke blue and bright,
With glancing sun and glancing spray,
As o'er the swell our boat made way,
As gallant as a gull in flight.

But, as we neared the lonely Isle
And look'd up at the naked height,
And saw the lighthouse towering white
With blinded lantern that all night

Had never shot a spark
Of comfort through the dark,
So ghostly in the cold sunlight
It seem'd, that we were struck the while
With wonder all too dread for words.
And, as into the tiny creek
We stole, beneath the hanging crag
We saw three queer, black, ugly birds—
Too big by far, in my belief,
For guillemot or shag—
Like seamen sitting bolt-upright
Upon a half-tide reef:
But as we neared they plunged from sight
Without a sound or spurt of white,
And still too mazed to speak,
We landed and made fast the boat
And climbed the track in single file
Each wishing he was safe afloat
On any sea, however far,
So it be far from Flannan Isle:
And still we seemed to climb, and climb
As though we'd lost all count of time
And so must climb for evermore;
Yet, all too soon, we reached the door—
The black, sun-blister'd lighthouse-door
That gaped for us ajar.

As on the threshold for a spell
We paused, we seem'd to breathe the smell
Of limewash and of tar,
Familiar as our daily breath,
As though 'twere some strange scent of death;
And so, yet wondering, side by side,
We stood a moment, still tongue-tied,

And each with black foreboding eyed
The door ere we should fling it wide
To leave the sunlight for the gloom:
Till, plucking courage up, at last,
Hard on each other's heels we passed
Into the living-room.

Yet as we crowded through the door
We only saw a table spread
For dinner, meat and cheese and bread,
But all untouched, and no one there:
As though, when they sat down to eat,
Ere they could even taste,
Alarm had come and they in haste
Had risen and left the bread and meat,
For at the table-head a chair
Lay tumbled on the floor.

We listened; but we only heard
The feeble cheeping of a bird
That starved upon its perch;
And, listening still, without a word
We set about our hopeless search.
We hunted high, we hunted low,
And soon ransack'd the empty house;
Then o'er the Island to and fro
We ranged, to listen and to look
In every cranny, cleft or nook
That might have hid a bird or mouse:
But, though we search'd from shore to shore
We found no sign in any place,
And soon again stood face to face
Before the gaping door,
And stole into the room once more

As frighten'd children steal.
Ay, though we hunted high and low
And hunted everywhere,
Of the three men's fate we found no trace
Of any kind in any place,
But a door ajar and an untouched meal
And an overtoppled chair.

And as we listened in the gloom
Of that forsaken living-room—
A chill clutch on our breath—
We thought how ill-chance came to all
Who kept the Flannan Light,
And how the rock had been the death
Of many a likely lad—

How six had come to a sudden end
And three had gone stark mad,
And one, whom we'd all known as friend,
Had leapt from the lantern one still night
And fallen dead by the lighthouse wall—
And long we thought
On the three we sought,
And of what might yet befall.

Like curs a glance has brought to heel
We listen'd, flinching there,
And looked and looked on the untouch'd meal
And the overtoppled chair.

We seem'd to stand for an endless while,
Though still no word was said,
Three men alive on Flannan Isle
Who thought on three men dead.

W. W. GIBSON

PART I

An ancient
Mariner
meeteth three
Gallants
bidden to a
wedding-feast,
and detaineth
one.

IT is an ancient Mariner
And he stoppeth one of three.
'By thy long grey beard and glittering eye,
Now wherefore stopp'st thou me?

The Bridegroom's doors are opened wide,
And I am next of kin;
The guests are met, the feast is set:
May'st hear the merry din.'

He holds him with his skinny hand,
'There was a ship,' quoth he.
'Hold off! unhand me, grey-beard loon!'
Eftsoons his hand dropt he.

The Wedding-
Guest is spell-
bound by the
eye of the old
seafaring man,
and constrained
to hear his tale.

He holds him with his glittering eye—
The Wedding-Guest stood still,
And listens like a three years' child:
The Mariner hath his will.

The Wedding-Guest sat on a stone:
He cannot choose but hear;
And thus spake on that ancient man,
The bright-eyed Mariner.

'The ship was cheered, the harbour cleared,
Merrily did we drop
Below the kirk, below the hill,
Below the lighthouse top.

The Mariner
tells how the
ship sailed
southward with
a good wind
and fair
weather, till
it reached the
Line.

The Sun came up upon the left,
Out of the sea came he!
And he shone bright, and on the right
Went down into the sea.

Higher and higher every day,
Till over the mast at noon——'
The Wedding-Guest here beat his breast,
For he heard the loud bassoon.

The Wedding-
Guest heareth
the bridal
music; but the
Mariner con-
tinueth his tale.

The bride hath paced into the hall,
Red as a rose is she;
Nodding their heads before her goes
The merry minstrelsy.

The Wedding-Guest he beat his breast,
Yet he cannot choose but hear;
And thus spake on that ancient man,
The bright-eyed Mariner:

The ship driven
by a storm to-
ward the South
Pole.

'And now the STORM-BLAST came, and he
Was tyrannous and strong:
He struck with his o'ertaking wings,
And chased us south along.

With sloping masts and dipping prow,
As who pursued with yell and blow
Still treads the shadow of his foe,
And forward bends his head,
The ship drove fast, loud roared the blast,
And southward aye we fled.

And now there came both mist and snow
And it grew wondrous cold:
And ice, mast-high, came floating by,
As green as emerald.

The land of ice, and of fearful sounds where no living thing was to be seen.

And through the drifts the snowy clifts
Did send a dismal sheen:
Nor shapes of men nor beasts we ken—
The ice was all between.

The ice was here, the ice was there,
The ice was all around:
It cracked and growled, and roared and howled,
Like noises in a swound!

Till a great sea-bird, called the Albatross, came through the snow-fog, and was received with great joy and hospitality.

At length did cross an Albatross,
Thorough the fog it came;
As if it had been a Christian soul,
We hailed it in God's name.

It ate the food it ne'er had eat,
And round and round it flew.
The ice did split with a thunder-fit;
The helmsman steered us through!

And lo! the Albatross proveth a bird of good omen, and followeth the ship as it returned northward through fog and floating ice.

And a good south wind sprung up behind;
The Albatross did follow,
And every day, for food or play,
Came to the mariners' hollo!

In mist or cloud, on mast or shroud,
It perched for vespers nine;
Whiles all the night, through fog-smoke white,
Glimmered the white moonshine.'

The ancient Mariner inhospitably killeth the pious bird of good omen.

'God save thee, ancient Mariner,
From the fiends that plague thee thus!—
Why look'st thou so?'—'With my crossbow
I shot the ALBATROSS.

71

PART II

The Sun now rose upon the right:
Out of the sea came he,
Still hid in mist, and on the left
Went down into the sea.

And the good south wind still blew behind,
But no sweet bird did follow,
Nor any day for food or play
Came to the mariners' hollo!

His shipmates cry out against the ancient Mariner for killing the bird of good luck.

And I had done a hellish thing,
And it would work 'em woe:
For all averred, I had killed the bird
That made the breeze to blow.
Ah wretch! said they, the bird to slay,
That made the breeze to blow!

But when the fog cleared off, they justify the same, and thus make themselves accomplices in the crime.

Nor dim nor red, like God's own head,
The glorious Sun uprist:
Then all averred, I had killed the bird
That brought the fog and mist.
'Twas right, said they, such birds to slay,
That bring the fog and mist.

The fair breeze continues; the ship enters the Pacific Ocean, and sails northward, even till it reaches the Line.

The fair breeze blew, the white foam flew,
The furrow followed free;
We were the first that ever burst
Into that silent sea.

The ship hath been suddenly becalmed.

Down dropt the breeze, the sails dropt down,
'Twas sad as sad could be;
And we did speak only to break
The silence of the sea!

All in a hot and copper sky,
The bloody Sun, at noon,
Right up above the mast did stand,
No bigger than the Moon.

Day after day, day after day,
We stuck, nor breath nor motion;
As idle as a painted ship
Upon a painted ocean.

And the Albatross begins to be avenged.

Water, water, everywhere,
And all the boards did shrink;
Water, water, everywhere,
Nor any drop to drink.

The very deep did rot: O Christ!
That ever this should be!
Yea, slimy things did crawl with legs
Upon the slimy sea.

About, about, in reel and rout,
The death-fires danced at night;
The water, like a witch's oils,
Burnt green, and blue, and white.

And some in dreams assurèd were
Of the Spirit that plagued us so;
Nine fathoms deep he had followed us
From the land of mist and snow.

A Spirit had followed them; one of the invisible inhabitants of this planet, neither departed souls nor angels; concerning whom the learned Jew, Josephus, and the Platonic Constantinopolitan, Michael Psellus, may be consulted. They are very numerous, and there is no climate or element without one or more.

73

And every tongue, through utter drought,
Was withered at the root;
We could not speak, no more than if
We had been choked with soot.

Ah! well-a-day! what evil looks
Had I from old and young!
Instead of the cross, the Albatross
About my neck was hung.

PART III

There passed a weary time. Each throat
Was parched, and glazed each eye.
A weary time! a weary time!
How glazed each weary eye,
When looking westward, I beheld
A something in the sky.

At first it seemed a little speck,
And then it seemed a mist;
It moved and moved, and took at last
A certain shape, I wist.

A speck, a mist, a shape, I wist!
And still it neared and neared:
As if it dodged a water-sprite,
It plunged, and tacked, and veered.

With throats unslaked, with black lips baked,
We could nor laugh nor wail;
Through utter drought all dumb we stood!
I bit my arm, I sucked the blood,
And cried, A sail! a sail!

With throats unslaked, with black lips baked,
Agape they heard me call:

A flash of joy;

Gramercy! they for joy did grin,
And all at once their breath drew in,
As they were drinking all.

And horror follows. For can it be a ship that comes onward without wind or tide?

See! See! (I cried) she tacks no more!
Hither to work us weal,
Without a breeze, without a tide,
She steadies with upright keel!

The western wave was all aflame,
The day was well nigh done!
Almost upon the western wave
Rested the broad bright Sun;
When that strange shape drove suddenly
Betwixt us and the Sun.

It seemeth him but the skeleton of a ship.

And straight the Sun was flecked with bars
(Heaven's Mother send us grace!),
As if through a dungeon-grate he peered
With broad and burning face.

Alas! (thought I, and my heart beat loud),
How fast she nears and nears!
Are those her sails that glance in the Sun,
Like restless gossameres?

And its ribs are seen as bars on the face of the setting Sun. The Spectre-Woman and her Death-mate, and no other, on board the skeleton ship. Like vessel, like crew!

Are those her ribs through which the Sun
Did peer, as through a grate?
And is that Woman all her crew?
Is that a DEATH? and are there two?
Is DEATH that Woman's mate?

75

Her lips were red, her looks were free,
Her locks were yellow as gold:
Her skin was as white as leprosy,
The Night-mare LIFE-IN-DEATH was she,
Who thicks man's blood with cold.

Death and Life-in-Death have diced for the ship's crew, and she (the latter) winneth the ancient Mariner.

The naked hulk alongside came,
And the twain were casting dice;
'The game is done! I've won! I've won!'
Quoth she, and whistles thrice.

No twilight within the courts of the Sun.

The Sun's rim dips; the stars rush out:
At one stride comes the dark;
With far-heard whisper, o'er the sea,
Off shot the spectre-bark.

We listened and looked sideways up!
Fear at my heart, as at a cup,
My life-blood seemed to sip!
The stars were dim, and thick the night,
The steersman's face by his lamp gleamed
white;
From the sails the dew did drip—

At the rising of the Moon,

Till clomb above the eastern bar
The hornèd Moon, with one bright star
Within the nether tip.

One after another,

One after one, by the star-dogged Moon,
Too quick for groan or sigh,
Each turned his face with a ghastly pang,
And cursed me with his eye.

Four times fifty living men,
(And I heard nor sigh nor groan),
With heavy thump, a lifeless lump,
They dropped down one by one.

The souls did from their bodies fly—
They fled to bliss or woe!
And every soul, it passed me by
Like the whizz of my cross-bow!'

PART IV

The Wedding-
Guest feareth
that a spirit
is talking to
him.
'I fear thee, ancient Mariner!
I fear thy skinny hand!
And thou art long, and lank, and brown,
As is the ribbed sea-sand.

I fear thee and thy glittering eye,
And thy skinny hand so brown.'—
But the ancient
Mariner assur-
eth him of his
bodily life, and
proceedeth to
relate his hor-
rible penance.
'Fear not, fear not, thou Wedding-Guest!
This body dropt not down.

Alone, alone, all, all alone,
Alone on a wide, wide sea!
And never a saint took pity on
My soul in agony.

The many men, so beautiful!
And they all dead did lie:
And a thousand thousand slimy things
Lived on; and so did I.

I looked upon the rotting sea,
And drew my eyes away;
I looked upon the rotting deck,
And there the dead men lay.

I looked to heaven, and tried to pray;
But or ever a prayer had gusht,
A wicked whisper came, and made
My heart as dry as dust.

I closed my lids, and kept them close,
And the balls like pulses beat;
For the sky and the sea, and the sea and the
sky
Lay like a load on my weary eye,
And the dead were at my feet.

But the curse
liveth for him
in the eye of the
dead men.

The cold sweat melted from their limbs,
Nor rot nor reek did they:
The look with which they looked on me
Had never passed away.

An orphan's curse would drag to hell
A spirit from on high;
But oh! more horrible than that
Is the curse in a dead man's eye!
Seven days, seven nights, I saw that curse,
And yet I could not die.

In his loneli-
ness and
fixedness he
yearneth
towards the
journeying
Moon, and the

The moving Moon went up the sky,
And nowhere did abide;
Softly she was going up,
And a star or two beside—

stars that still sojourn, yet still move onward; and everywhere the blue sky
belongs to them, and is their appointed rest and their native country and their
own natural homes, which they enter unannounced, as lords that are certainly
expected and yet there is a silent joy at their arrival.

Her beams bemocked the sultry main,
Like April hoar-frost spread;
But where the ship's huge shadow lay,
The charmèd water burnt alway
A still and awful red.

Beyond the shadow of the ship,
I watched the water-snakes:
They moved in tracks of shining white,
And when they reared, the elfish light
Fell off in hoary flakes.

Within the shadow of the ship
I watched their rich attire:
Blue, glossy green, and velvet black,
They coiled and swam; and every track
Was a flash of golden fire.

O happy living things! no tongue
Their beauty might declare:
A spring of love gushed from my heart,
And I blessed them unaware:
Sure my kind saint took pity on me,
And I blessed them unaware.

The self-same moment I could pray;
And from my neck so free
The Albatross fell off, and sank
Like lead into the sea.

PART V

Oh sleep! it is a gentle thing,
Beloved from pole to pole!
To Mary Queen the praise be given!
She sent the gentle sleep from Heaven,
That slid into my soul.

By grace of
the holy
Mother, the
ancient
Mariner is
refreshed
with rain.

The silly buckets on the deck,
That had so long remained,
I dreamt that they were filled with dew;
And when I awoke, it rained.

My lips were wet, my throat was cold,
My garments all were dank;
Sure I had drunken in my dreams,
And still my body drank.

I moved, and could not feel my limbs:
I was so light—almost
I thought that I had died in sleep,
And was a blessèd ghost.

He heareth
sounds and
seeth strange
sights and
commotions
in the sky and
the element.

And soon I heard a roaring wind:
It did not come anear;
But with its sound it shook the sails,
That were so thin and sere.

The upper air burst into life!
And a hundred fire-flags sheen;
To and fro they were hurried about!
And to and fro, and in and out,
The wan stars danced between.

And the coming wind did roar more loud,
And the sails did sigh like sedge;
And the rain poured down from one black
  cloud;
The Moon was at its edge.

The thick black cloud was cleft, and still
The Moon was at its side:
Like waters shot from some high crag,
The lightning fell with never a jag,
A river steep and wide.

The bodies of
the ship's crew
are inspired,
and the ship
moves on;
The loud wind never reached the ship,
Yet now the ship moved on!
Beneath the lightning and the Moon
The dead men gave a groan.

They groaned, they stirred, they all uprose,
Nor spake, nor moved their eyes;
It had been strange, even in a dream,
To have seen those dead men rise.

The helmsman steered, the ship moved on;
Yet never a breeze up-blew;
The mariners all 'gan work the ropes,
Where they were wont to do;
They raised their limbs like lifeless tools—
We were a ghastly crew.

The body of my brother's son
Stood by me, knee to knee:
The body and I pulled at one rope,
But he said naught to me.'

But not by
the souls of
the men, nor
by demons of
earth or middle
air, but by a
blessed troop
of angelic
spirits, sent
down by the
invocation of
the guardian
saint.

'I fear thee, ancient Mariner!'
'Be calm, thou Wedding-Guest!
'Twas not those souls that fled in pain,
Which to their corses came again,
But a troop of spirits blest:

For when it dawned—they dropt their arms,
And clustered round the mast;
Sweet sounds rose slowly through their mouths,
And from their bodies passed.

Around, around, flew each sweet sound,
Then darted to the Sun;
Slowly the sounds came back again,
Now mixed, now one by one.

Sometimes a-dropping from the sky
I heard the sky-lark sing;
Sometimes all little birds that are,
How they seemed to fill the sea and air
With their sweet jargoning!

And now 'twas like all instruments,
Now like a lonely flute;
And now it is an angel's song,
That makes the heavens be mute.

It ceased; yet still the sails made on
A pleasant noise till noon,
A noise like of a hidden brook
In the leafy month of June,
That to the sleeping woods all night
Singeth a quiet tune.

Till noon we quietly sailed on,
Yet never a breeze did breathe:
Slowly and smoothly went the ship,
Moved onward from beneath.

Under the keel nine fathom deep,
From the land of mist and snow,
The spirit slid: and it was he
That made the ship to go.
The sails at noon left off their tune,
And the ship stood still also.

The Sun, right up above the mast,
Had fixed her to the ocean:
But in a minute she 'gan stir,
With a short, uneasy motion—
Backwards and forwards half her length
With a short uneasy motion.

Then like a pawing horse let go,
She made a sudden bound:
It flung the blood into my head,
And I fell down in a swound.

How long in that same fit I lay,
I have not to declare;
But ere my living life returned,
I heard, and in my soul discerned
Two voices in the air.

'Is it he?' quoth one, 'Is this the man?
By him who died on cross,
With his cruel bow he laid full low
The harmless Albatross.

The spirit who bideth by himself
In the land of mist and snow,
He loved the bird that loved the man
Who shot him with his bow.'

The other was a softer voice,
As soft as honey-dew:
Quoth he, 'The man hath penance done,
And penance more will do.'

PART VI

First Voice:
'But tell me, tell me! speak again,
Thy soft response renewing—
What makes that ship drive on so fast?
What is the ocean doing?'

Second Voice:
'Still as a slave before his lord,
The ocean hath no blast;
His great bright eye most silently
Up to the Moon is cast—

If he may know which way to go;
For she guides him smooth or grim.
See, brother, see! how graciously
She looketh down on him.'

The Mariner
hath been cast
into a trance;
for the angelic
power causeth
the vessel to
drive north-
ward faster
than human
life could
endure.

First Voice:
'But why drives on that ship so fast,
Without or wave or wind?'

Second Voice:
'The air is cut away before,
And closes from behind.

Fly, brother, fly! more high, more high!
Or we shall be belated:
For slow and slow that ship will go,
When the Mariner's trance is abated.'

The super-
natural motion
is retarded;
the Mariner
awakes, and
his penance
begins anew.
I woke, and we were sailing on
As in a gentle weather:
'Twas night, calm night, the Moon was high;
The dead men stood together.

All stood together on the deck,
For a charnel-dungeon fitter:
All fixed on me their stony eyes,
That in the Moon did glitter.

The pang, the curse, with which they died,
Had never passed away:
I could not draw my eyes from theirs,
Nor turn them up to pray.

The curse is fin-
ally expiated.
And now this spell was snapt: once more
I viewed the ocean green,
And looked far forth, yet little saw
Of what had else been seen—

Like one, that on a lonesome road
Doth walk in fear and dread,
And having once turned round walks on,
And turns no more his head;
Because he knows a frightful fiend
Doth close behind him tread.

But soon there breathed a wind on me,
Nor sound nor motion made:
Its path was not upon the sea,
In ripple or in shade.

It raised my hair, it fanned my cheek
Like a meadow-gale of spring—
It mingled strangely with my fears,
Yet it felt like a welcoming.

Swiftly, swiftly flew the ship,
Yet she sailed softly too:
Sweetly, sweetly blew the breeze—
On me alone it blew.

And the ancient Mariner beholdeth his native country.

Oh! dream of joy! is this indeed
The lighthouse top I see?
Is this the hill? is this the kirk?
Is this mine own countree?

We drifted o'er the harbour-bar,
And I with sobs did pray—
O let me be awake, my God!
Or let me sleep alway.

The harbour-bar was clear as glass,
So smoothly it was strewn!
And on the bay the moonlight lay,
And the shadow of the Moon.

The rock shone bright, the kirk no less,
That stands above the rock:
The moonlight steeped in silentness
The steady weathercock.

And the bay was white with silent light,
Till rising from the same,
Full many shapes, that shadows were,
In crimson colours came.

And appear in
their own forms
of light.
A little distance from the prow
Those crimson shadows were:
I turn'd my eyes upon the deck—
Oh, Christ! what saw I there!

Each corse lay flat, lifeless and flat,
And, by the holy rood!
A man all light, a seraph-man,
On every corse there stood.

This seraph-band, each waved his hand:
It was a heavenly sight!
They stood as signals to the land,
Each one a lovely light;

This seraph-band, each waved his hand,
No voice did they impart—
No voice; but Oh! the silence sank
Like music on my heart.

But soon I heard the dash of oars,
I heard the Pilot's cheer;
My head was turned perforce away,
And I saw a boat appear.

The Pilot and the Pilot's boy,
I heard them coming fast:
Dear Lord in Heaven! it was a joy
The dead men could not blast.

I saw a third—I heard his voice:
It is the Hermit good!
He singeth loud his godly hymns
That he makes in the wood.
He'll shrieve my soul, he'll wash away
The Albatross's blood.

PART VII

The Hermit
of the Wood,
This hermit good lives in that wood
Which slopes down to the sea.
How loudly his sweet voice he rears!
He loves to talk with mariners
That come from a far countree.

He kneels at morn, and noon, and eve—
He hath a cushion plump:
It is the moss that wholly hides
The rotted old oak-stump.

The skiff-boat neared: I heard them talk,
'Why, this is strange, I trow!
Where are those lights so many and fair,
That signal made but now?'

Approacheth
the ship with
wonder.
'Strange, by my faith!' the Hermit said—
'And they answered not our cheer!
The planks look warped! and see those sails,
How thin they are and sere!
I never saw aught like to them,
Unless perchance it were

88

Brown skeletons of leaves that lag
My forest-brook along;
When the ivy-tod is heavy with snow,
And the owlet whoops to the wolf below,
That eats the she-wolf's young.'

'Dear Lord! it hath a fiendish look'—
(The Pilot made reply)
'I am a-feared.'—'Push on, push on!'
Said the Hermit cheerily.

The boat came closer to the ship,
But I nor spake nor stirred;
The boat came close beneath the ship,
And straight a sound was heard.

The ship suddenly sinketh.

Under the water it rumbled on,
Still louder and more dread:
It reached the ship, it split the bay;
The ship went down like lead.

The ancient Mariner is saved in the Pilot's boat.

Stunned by that loud and dreadful sound,
Which sky and ocean smote,
Like one that hath been seven days drowned
My body lay afloat;
But swift as dreams, myself I found
Within the Pilot's boat.

Upon the whirl, where sank the ship,
The boat spun round and round;
And all was still, save that the hill
Was telling of the sound.

I moved my lips—the Pilot shrieked
And fell down in a fit;
The holy Hermit raised his eyes,
And prayed where he did sit.

I took the oars: the Pilot's boy,
Who now doth crazy go,
Laughed loud and long, and all the while
His eyes went to and fro.
'Ha! Ha!' quoth he, 'full plain I see,
The Devil knows how to row.'

And now, all in my own countree,
I stood on the firm land!
The Hermit stepped forth from the boat,
And scarcely he could stand.

'O shrieve me, shrieve me, holy man!'
The Hermit crossed his brow.
'Say quick,' quoth he, 'I bid thee say—
What manner of man art thou?'

Forthwith this frame of mine was wrenched
With a woeful agony,
Which forced me to begin my tale;
And then it left me free.

Since then, at an uncertain hour,
That agony returns:
And till my ghastly tale is told,
This heart within me burns.

constraineth
him to travel
from land to
land;

I pass, like night, from land to land;
I have strange power of speech;
That moment that his face I see,
I know the man that must hear me:
To him my tale I teach.

What loud uproar bursts from that door!
The wedding-guests are there:
But in the garden-bower the bride
And bride-maids singing are:
And hark, the little vesper bell,
Which biddeth me to prayer!

O Wedding-Guest! this soul hath been
Alone on a wide wide sea:
So lonely 'twas, that God Himself
Scarce seemèd there to be.

O sweeter than the marriage-feast,
'Tis sweeter far to me,
To walk together to the kirk
With a goodly company!—

To walk together to the kirk,
And all together pray,
While each to his great Father bends,
Old men, and babes, and loving friends,
And youths and maidens gay!

And to teach,
by his own
example, love
and reverence
to all things
that God made
and loveth.

Farewell, farewell! but this I tell
To thee, thou Wedding-Guest!
He prayeth well, who loveth well
Both man and bird and beast.

He prayeth best, who loveth best
All things both great and small;
For the dear God who loveth us,
He made and loveth all.'

The Mariner, whose eye is bright,
Whose beard with age is hoar,
Is gone: and now the Wedding-Guest
Turned from the bridegroom's door.

He went like one that hath been stunned.
And is of sense forlorn:
A sadder and a wiser man,
He rose the morrow morn.

S. T. COLERIDGE

35   *When I set out for Lyonnesse*

WHEN I set out for Lyonnesse,
　A hundred miles away,
　The rime was on the spray,
And starlight lit my lonesomeness
When I set out for Lyonnesse
　A hundred miles away.

What would bechance at Lyonnesse
　While I should sojourn there
　No prophet durst declare,
Nor did the wisest wizard guess
What would bechance at Lyonnesse
　While I should sojourn there.

When I came back from Lyonnesse
　With magic in my eyes,
　All marked with mute surmise
My radiance rare and fathomless,
When I came back from Lyonnesse
　With magic in my eyes!

THOMAS HARDY

36   *The Oxen*

CHRISTMAS Eve, and twelve of the clock.
　'Now they are all on their knees,'
An elder said as we sat in a flock
　By the embers in hearthside ease.

We pictured the meek mild creatures where
　They dwelt in their strawy pen,
Nor did it occur to one of us there
　To doubt they were kneeling then.

So fair a fancy few would weave
　In these years! Yet, I feel,
If someone said on Christmas Eve,
　'Come; see the oxen kneel

'In the lonely barton by yonder coomb
　Our childhood used to know,'
I should go with him in the gloom,
　Hoping it might be so.

THOMAS HARDY

THE sheets were frozen hard, and they cut the naked hand;
The decks were like a slide where a seaman scarce could
 stand;
The wind was a nor'wester, blowing squally off the sea;
And cliffs and spouting breakers were the only things a-lee.

They heard the surf a-roaring before the break of day;
But 'twas only with the peep of light we saw how ill we lay.
We tumbled every hand on deck instanter, with a shout,
And we gave her the maintops'l, and stood by to go about.

All day we tacked and tacked between the South Head and
 the North;
All day we hauled the frozen sheets, and got no further forth;
All day as cold as charity, in bitter pain and dread,
For very life and nature we tacked from head to head.

We gave the South a wider berth, for there the tide-race
 roared;
But every tack we made we brought the North Head close
 aboard:
So's we saw the cliffs and houses, and the breakers running
 high,
And the coastguard in his garden, with his glass against his
 eye.

The frost was on the village roofs as white as ocean foam;
The good red fires were burning bright in every 'longshore
 home;
The windows sparkled clear, and the chimneys volleyed out;
And I vow we sniffed the victuals as the vessel went about.

The bells upon the church were rung with a mighty jovial
    cheer;
For it's just that I should tell you how (of all days in the
    year)
This day of our adversity was blessèd Christmas morn,
And the house above the coastguard's was the house where I
    was born.

O well I saw the pleasant room, the pleasant faces there,
My mother's silver spectacles, my father's silver hair;
And well I saw the firelight, like a flight of homely elves,
Go dancing round the china plates that stand upon the
    shelves.

And well I knew the talk they had, the talk that was of me,
Of the shadow on the household and the son that went to sea;
And O the wicked fool I seemed, in every kind of way,
To be here and hauling frozen ropes on blessèd Christmas
    Day.

They lit the high sea-light, and the dark began to fall,
'All hands to loose topgallant sails,' I heard the captain call.
'By the Lord, she'll never stand it,' our first mate Jackson,
    cried,
. . . 'It's the one way or the other, Mr. Jackson,' he replied.

She staggered to her bearings, but the sails were new and
    good,
And the ship smelt up to windward just as though she
    understood.
As the winter's day was ending, in the entry of the night,
We cleared the weary headland, and passed below the light.

And they heaved a mighty breath, every soul on board but
    me,
As they saw her nose again pointing handsome out to sea;
But all that I could think of, in the darkness and the cold,
Was just that I was leaving home and my folks were growing
    old.

R. L. STEVENSON

38   *Carol*

I SING of a Maiden
    That is makeless;
King of all Kings
    To her son she ches.

He came al so still
    There his mother was,
As dew in April
    That falleth on the grass.

He came al so still
    To his mother's bour,
As dew in April
    That falleth on the flour.

He came al so still
    There his mother lay,
As dew in April
    That falleth on the spray.

Mother and maiden
    Was never none but she:
Well may such a lady
    Goddes mother be.

ANON.

makeless, peerless.   *ches*, chose.

Ring Out, Wild Bells

RING out, wild bells, to the wild sky,
  The flying cloud, the frosty light:
  The year is dying in the night;
Ring out, wild bells, and let him die.

Ring out the old, ring in the new,
  Ring, happy bells, across the snow:
  The year is going, let him go;
Ring out the false, ring in the true.

Ring out the grief that saps the mind,
  For those that here we see no more;
  Ring out the feud of rich and poor,
Ring in redress to all mankind.

Ring out a slowly dying cause,
  And ancient forms of party strife;
  Ring in the nobler modes of life,
With sweeter manners, purer laws.

Ring out the want, the care, the sin,
  The faithless coldness of the times;
  Ring out, ring out my mournful rhymes,
But ring the fuller minstrel in.

Ring out false pride in place and blood,
  The civic slander and the spite;
  Ring in the love of truth and right,
Ring in the common love of good.

Ring out old shapes of foul disease;
   Ring out the narrowing lust of gold;
   Ring out the thousand wars of old,
Ring in the thousand years of peace.

Ring in the valiant man and free,
   The larger heart, the kindlier hand;
   Ring out the darkness of the land,
Ring in the Christ that is to be.

LORD TENNYSON

40   *Winter the Huntsman*

THROUGH his iron glades
Rides Winter the Huntsman,
All colour fades
As his horn is heard sighing.

Far through the forest
His wild hooves crash and thunder
Till many a mighty branch
Is torn asunder.

And the red reynard creeps
To his hole near the river,
The copper leaves fall
And the bare trees shiver.

As night creeps from the ground,
Hides each tree from its brother,
And each dying sound
Reveals yet another.

Is it Winter the Huntsman
Who gallops through his iron glades,
Cracking his cruel whip
To the gathering shades?

OSBERT SITWELL

41 *Gipsies*

THE snow falls deep; the forest lies alone;
The boy goes hasty for his load of brakes,
Then thinks upon the fire and hurries back;
The gipsy knocks his hands and tucks them up,
And seeks his squalid camp, half hid in snow,
Beneath the oak which breaks away the wind,
And bushes close in snow-like hovel warm;
There tainted mutton wastes upon the coals,
And the half-wasted dog squats close and rubs,
Then feels the heat too strong, and goes aloof;
He watches well, but none a bit can spare,
And vainly waits the morsel thrown away.
'Tis thus they live—a picture to the place,
A quiet, pilfering, unprotected race.

JOHN CLARE

42 *Under the Greenwood Tree*

UNDER the greenwood tree
Who loves to lie with me,
And tune his merry note
Unto the sweet bird's throat,
Come hither, come hither, come hither:
Here shall he see
No enemy
But winter and rough weather.

Who doth ambition shun
And loves to live i' th' sun,
Seeking the food he eats
And pleas'd with what he gets,
Come hither, come hither, come hither:
Here shall he see
No enemy
But winter and rough weather.

W. SHAKESPEARE

43   *A Runnable Stag*

WHEN the pods went pop on the broom, green broom,
And apples began to be golden-skinned,
We harboured a stag in the Priory coomb,
And we feathered his trail up-wind, up-wind,
We feathered his trail up-wind—
A stag of warrant, a stag, a stag,
A runnable stag, a kingly crop,
Brow, bay and tray and three on top,
A stag, a runnable stag.

Then the huntsman's horn rang yap, yap, yap,
And 'Forwards' we heard the harbourer shout;
But 'twas only a brocket that broke a gap
In the beechen underwood, driven out,
From the underwood antlered out
By warrant and might of the stag, the stag,
The runnable stag, whose lordly mind
Was bent on sleep, though beamed and tined
He stood, a runnable stag.

So we tufted the covert till afternoon
  With Tinkerman's Pup and Bell-of-the-North;
And hunters were sulky and hounds out of tune
  Before we tufted the right stag forth,
  Before we tufted him forth,
    The stag of warrant, the wily stag,
    The runnable stag with his kingly crop,
    Brow, bay and tray and three on top,
    The royal and runnable stag.

It was Bell-of-the-North and Tinkerman's Pup
  That stuck to the scent till the copse was drawn.
'Tally ho! tally ho!' and the hunt was up,
  The tufters whipped and the pack laid on,
  The resolute pack laid on,
    And the stag of warrant away at last,
    The runnable stag, the same, the same,
    His hoofs on fire, his horns like flame,
    A stag, a runnable stag.

'Let your gelding be: if you check or chide
  He stumbles at once and you're out of the hunt;
For three hundred gentlemen, able to ride,
  On hunters accustomed to bear the brunt,
  Accustomed to bear the brunt,
    Are after the runnable stag, the stag,
    The runnable stag with his kingly crop,
    Brow, bay and tray and three on top,
    The right, the runnable stag.'

By perilous paths in coomb and dell,
  The heather, the rocks, and the river-bed,
The pace grew hot, for the scent lay well,
  And a runnable stag goes right ahead,
  The quarry went right ahead—

Ahead, ahead, and fast and far;
His antlered crest, his cloven hoof,
Brow, bay and tray and three aloof,
The stag, the runnable stag.

For a matter of twenty miles and more,
    By the densest hedge and the highest wall,
Through herds of bullocks he baffled the lore
    Of harbourer, huntsman, hounds and all,
    Of harbourer, hounds and all—
        The stag of warrant, the wily stag,
        For twenty miles, and five and five,
        He ran, and he never was caught alive,
        This stag, this runnable stag.

When he turned at bay in the leafy gloom,
    In the emerald gloom where the brook ran deep,
He heard in the distance the rollers boom,
    And he saw in a vision of peaceful sleep,
    In a wonderful vision of sleep,
        A stag of warrant, a stag, a stag,
        A runnable stag in a jewelled bed,
        Under the sheltering ocean dead,
        A stag, a runnable stag.

So a fateful hope lit up his eye,
    And he opened his nostrils wide again,
And he tossed his branching antlers high
    As he headed the hunt down the Charlock glen,
    As he raced down the echoing glen
        For five miles more, the stag, the stag,
        For twenty miles, and five and five,
        Not to be caught now, dead or alive,
        The stag, the runnable stag.

Three hundred gentlemen, able to ride,
   Three hundred horses as gallant and free,
Beheld him escape on the evening tide,
   Far out till he sank in the Severn Sea,
   Till he sank in the depths of the sea—
      The stag, the buoyant stag, the stag
      That slept at last in a jewelled bed
      Under the sheltering ocean spread,
      The stag, the runnable stag.

JOHN DAVIDSON

44   *My Heart's in the Highlands*

MY heart's in the Highlands, my heart is not here;
My heart's in the Highlands a-chasing the deer;
Chasing the wild deer, and following the roe;
My heart's in the Highlands, wherever I go.
Farewell to the Highlands, farewell to the North,
The birthplace of valour, the country of worth;
Wherever I wander, wherever I rove,
The hills of the Highlands for ever I love.

Farewell to the mountains, high-covered with snow;
Farewell to the straths and green valleys below;
Farewell to the forests and wild-hanging woods;
Farewell to the torrents and loud-pouring floods.
My heart's in the Highlands, my heart is not here;
My heart's in the Highlands a-chasing the deer;
Chasing the wild deer, and following the roe;
My heart's in the Highlands, wherever I go.

ROBERT BURNS

45 *Lord Gorbals*

ONCE, as old Lord Gorbals motored
    Round his moors near John o' Groats,
He collided with a goatherd
    And a herd of forty goats.
By the time his car got through
They were all defunct but two.

Roughly he addressed the goatherd:
    'Dash my whiskers and my corns!
Can't you teach your goats, you dotard,
    That they ought to sound their horns?
Look, my A.A. badge is bent!
I've a mind to raise your rent!'
                    HARRY GRAHAM

46 *The Hippopotamus*

I SHOOT the Hippopotamus
With bullets made of platinum,
Because if I use leaden ones
His hide is sure to flatten 'em.
                    HILAIRE BELLOC

47 *The Bull*

SEE an old unhappy bull,
Sick in soul and body both,
Slouching in the undergrowth
Of the forest beautiful,
Banished from the herd he led,
Bulls and cows a thousand head.

Cranes and gaudy parrots go
Up and down the burning sky;
Tree-top cats purr drowsily
In the dim-day green below;
And troops of monkeys, nutting, some,
All disputing, go and come;

And things abominable sit
Picking offal buck or swine,
On the mess and over it
Burnished flies and beetles shine,
And spiders big as bladders lie
Under hemlocks ten foot high;

And a dotted serpent curled
Round and round and round a tree,
Yellowing its greenery,
Keeps a watch on all the world,
All the world and this old bull
In the forest beautiful.

Bravely by his fall he came:
One he led, a bull of blood
Newly come to lustihood,
Fought and put his prince to shame,
Snuffed and pawed the prostrate head,
Tameless even while it bled.

There they left him, every one,
Left him there without a lick,
Left him for the birds to pick,
Left him there for carrion,
Vilely from their bosom cast
Wisdom, worth, and love at last.

When the lion left his lair
And roared his beauty through the hills,
And the vultures pecked their quills
And flew into the middle air,
Then this prince no more to reign
Came to life and lived again.

He snuffed the herd in far retreat,
He saw the blood upon the ground,
And snuffed the burning airs around
Still with beevish odours sweet,
While the blood ran down his head
And his mouth ran slaver red.

Pity him, this fallen chief,
All his splendour, all his strength,
All his body's breadth and length
Dwindled down with shame and grief,
Half the bull he was before,
Bones and leather, nothing more.

See him standing dewlap-deep
In the rushes at the lake,
Surly, stupid, half asleep,
Waiting for his heart to break
And the birds to join the flies
Feasting at his bloodshot eyes;

Standing with his head hung down
In a stupor, dreaming things:
Green savannas, jungles brown,
Battlefields and bellowings,
Bulls undone and lions dead
And vultures flapping overhead.

Dreaming things: of days he spent
With his mother gaunt and lean
In the valley warm and green,
Full of baby wonderment,
Blinking out of silly eyes
At a hundred mysteries;

Dreaming over once again
How he wandered with a throng
Of bulls and cows a thousand strong,
Wandered on from plain to plain,
Up the hill and down the dale,
Always at his mother's tail;

How he lagged behind the herd,
Lagged and tottered, weak of limb,
And she turned and ran to him,
Blaring at the loathly bird
Stationed always in the skies,
Waiting for the flesh that dies.

Dreaming maybe of a day
When her drained and drying paps
Turned him to the sweets and saps,
Richer fountains by the way,
And she left the bull she bore,
And he looked to her no more;

And his little frame grew stout,
And his little legs grew strong,
And the way was not so long;
And his little horns came out,
And he played at butting trees
And boulder-stones and tortoises,

Joined a game of knobby skulls
With the youngsters of his year,
All the other little bulls,
Learning both to bruise and bear,
Learning how to stand a shock
Like a little bull of rock.

Dreaming of a day less dim,
Dreaming of a time less far,
When the faint but certain star
Of destiny burned clear for him,
And a fierce and wild unrest
Broke the quiet of his breast,

And the gristles of his youth
Hardened in his comely pow,
And he came to fighting growth,
Beat his bull and won his cow,
And flew his tail and trampled off
Past the tallest, vain enough,

And curved about in splendour full,
And curved again and snuffed the airs
As who should say Come out who dares!
And all beheld a bull, a Bull,
And knew that here was surely one
That backed for no bull, fearing none.

And the leader of the herd
Looked and saw, and beat the ground,
And shook the forest with his sound,
Bellowed at the loathly bird
Stationed always in the skies
Waiting for the flesh that dies.

Dreaming, this old bull forlorn,
Surely dreaming of the hour
When he came to sultan power,
And they owned him master-horn,
Chiefest bull of all among
Bulls and cows a thousand strong;

And in all the tramping herd
Not a bull that barred his way,
Not a cow that said him nay,
Not a bull or cow that erred
In the furnace of his look
Dared a second, worse rebuke:

Not in all the forest wide,
Jungle, thicket, pasture, fen,
Not another dared him then,
Dared him and again defied;
Not a sovereign buck or boar
Came a second time for more;

Not a serpent that survived
Once the terrors of his hoof
Risked a second time reproof,
Came a second time and lived,
Not a serpent in its skin
Came again for discipline;

Not a leopard bright as flame,
Flashing fingerhooks of steel
That a wooden tree might feel,
Met his fury once and came
For a second reprimand,
Not a leopard in the land.

Not a lion of them all,
Not a lion of the hills,
Hero of a thousand kills,
Dared a second fight and fall,
Dared that ram terrific twice,
Paid a second time the price.

Pity him, this dupe of dream,
Leader of the herd again
Only in his daft old brain,
Once again the bull supreme
And bull enough to bear the part
Only in his tameless heart.

Pity him that he must wake;
Even now the swarm of flies
Blackening his bloodshot eyes
Bursts and blusters round the lake,
Scattered from the feast half-fed,
By great shadows overhead;

And the dreamer turns away
From his visionary herds
And his splendid yesterday,
Turns to meet the loathly birds
Flocking round him from the skies,
Waiting for the flesh that dies.

RALPH HODGSON

48 **The War Horse**

HAST thou given the horse strength? hast thou clothed his neck with thunder?

Canst thou make him afraid as a grasshopper? the glory of his nostrils is terrible.

He paweth in the valley, and rejoiceth in his strength: he goeth on to meet the armed men.

He mocketh at fear, and is not affrighted: neither turneth he back from the sword.

The quiver rattleth against him, the glittering spear and the shield.

He swalloweth the ground with fierceness and rage: neither believeth he that it is the sound of the trumpet.

He saith among the trumpets, Ha, ha; and he smelleth the battle afar off, the thunder of the captains, and the shouting.

THE BIBLE

49 **The Raiders**

LAST night a wind from Lammermoor came roaring up the
    glen
With the tramp of trooping horses and the laugh of reckless
    men,
And struck a mailed hand on the gate and cried in rebel glee:
'Come forth! Come forth, my Borderer, and ride the March
    with me!'

I said, 'Oh! Wind of Lammermoor, the night's too dark to
    ride,
And all the men that fill the glen are ghosts of men that
    died!

The floods are down in Bowmont Burn, the moss is fetlock-
    deep;
Go back, wild Wind of Lammermoor, to Lauderdale—and
    sleep!'

Out spoke the Wind of Lammermoor, 'We know the road
    right well,
The road that runs by Kale and Jed across the Carter Fell;
There is no man of all the men in this grey troop of mine
But blind might ride the Borderside from Teviothead to Tyne!'

The horses fretted on their bits and pawed the flints to fire,
The riders swung them to the South full-faced to their
    desire;
'Come!' said the Wind of Lammermoor, and spoke full
    scornfully,
'Have ye no pride to mount and ride your fathers' road with
    me?'

A roan horse to the gate they led, foam-flecked and travelled
    far,
A snorting roan that tossed his head and flashed his forehead
    star;
There came a sound of clashing steel, and hoof-tramp up the
    glen,
. . . And two by two we cantered through, a troop of ghostly
    men!

.   .   .   .

I know not if the farms we fired are burned to ashes yet!
I know not if the stirks grew tired before the stars were set!
I only know that late last night when northern winds blew
    free,
A troop of men rode up the glen and brought a horse for me!

W. H. OGILVIE

112

THE wind was a torrent of darkness among the gusty trees,
The moon was a ghostly galleon tossed upon cloudy seas,
The road was a ribbon of moonlight over the purple moor,
And the highwayman came riding—
       Riding—riding—
The highwayman came riding, up to the old inn-door.

He'd a French cocked-hat on his forehead, a bunch of lace at
    his chin,
A coat of the claret velvet, and breeches of brown doe-skin;
They fitted with never a wrinkle: his boots were up to the
    thigh!
And he rode with a jewelled twinkle,
       His pistol butts a-twinkle,
His rapier hilt a-twinkle, under the jewelled sky.

Over the cobbles he clattered and clashed in the dark inn-
    yard,
He tapped with his whip on the shutters, but all was locked
    and barred;
He whistled a tune to the window, and who should be
    waiting there
But the landlord's black-eyed daughter,
       Bess, the landlord's daughter,
Plaiting a dark red love-knot into her long black hair.

And dark in the dark old inn-yard a stable-wicket creaked
Where Tim the ostler listened; his face was white and peaked;
His eyes were hollows of madness, his hair like mouldy hay,
But he loved the landlord's daughter,
       The landlord's red-lipped daughter,
Dumb as a dog he listened, and he heard the robber say—

'One kiss, my bonny sweetheart, I'm after a prize to-night,
But I shall be back with the yellow gold before the morning
    light;
Yet, if they press me sharply, and harry me through the day,
Then look for me by moonlight,
      Watch for me by moonlight,
I'll come to thee by moonlight, though hell should bar the
    way.'

He rose upright in the stirrups; he scarce could reach her
    hand,
But she loosened her hair i' the casement! His face burnt
    like a brand
As the black cascade of perfume came tumbling over his
    breast;
And he kissed its waves in the moonlight,
      (Oh, sweet black waves in the moonlight!)
Then he tugged at his rein in the moonlight, and galloped
    away to the west.

He did not come in the dawning; he did not come at noon;
And out o' the tawny sunset, before the rise o' the moon,
When the road was a gipsy's ribbon, looping the purple
    moor,
A red-coat troop came marching—
      Marching—marching—
King George's men came marching, up to the old inn-door.

They said no word to the landlord, they drank his ale
    instead.
But they gagged his daughter and bound her to the foot of her
    narrow bed;

Two of them knelt at her casement, with muskets at their side!
There was death at every window;
        And hell at one dark window;
For Bess could see, through the casement, the road that *he*
    would ride.

They had tied her up to attention, with many a sniggering
    jest;
They had bound a musket beside her, with the muzzle
    beneath her breast!
'Now keep good watch!' and they kissed her.
        She heard the dead man say—
Look for me by moonlight;
        Watch for me by moonlight;
I'll come to thee by moonlight, though hell should bar the way!

She twisted her hands behind her; but all the knots held good!
She writhed her hands till her fingers were wet with sweat or
    blood!
They stretched and strained in the darkness, and the hours
    crawled by like years,
Till, now, on the stroke of midnight,
        Cold, on the stroke of midnight,
The tip of one finger touched it! The trigger at least was hers!

The tip of one finger touched it; she strove no more for the
    rest!
Up, she stood up to attention, with the muzzle between her
    breast,
She would not risk their hearing; she would not strive again;
For the road lay bare in the moonlight;
        Blank and bare in the moonlight;
And the blood of her veins in the moonlight throbbed to her
    love's refrain.

Tlot-tlot; tlot-tlot! Had they heard it? The horse-hoofs ring-
 ing clear;
Tlot-tlot, tlot-tlot, in the distance? Were they deaf that they
 did not hear?
Down the ribbon of moonlight, over the brow of the hill,
The highwayman came riding,
                    Riding, riding!
The red-coats looked to their priming! She stood up,
 straight and still.

Tlot-tlot, in the frosty silence! *Tlot-tlot,* in the echoing night!
Nearer he came and nearer! Her face was like a light!
Her eyes grew wide for a moment; she drew one last deep
 breath,
Then her finger moved in the moonlight,
             Her musket shattered the moonlight,
Shattered her breast in the moonlight and warned him—
 with her death.

He turned; he spurred to the west; he did not know who
 stood
Bowed, with her head o'er the musket, drenched with her
 own red blood!
Not till the dawn he heard it, and slowly blanched to hear
How Bess, the landlord's daughter,
             The landlord's black-eyed daughter,
Had watched for her love in the moonlight, and died in the
 darkness there.

Back, he spurred like a madman, shrieking a curse to the sky,
With the white road smoking behind him and his rapier
 brandished high!
Blood-red were his spurs i' the golden noon; wine-red was
 his velvet-coat;

When they shot him down on the highway,
　　Down like a dog on the highway,
And he lay in his blood on the highway, with a bunch of
　　lace at his throat.

　　.　　　.　　　.　　　.　　　.　　　.　　　.

And still of a winter's night, they say, when the wind is in the
　　trees,
When the moon is a ghostly galleon tossed upon cloudy seas,
When the road is a ribbon of moonlight over the purple moor,
A highwayman comes riding—
　　Riding—riding—
A highwayman comes riding, up to the old inn-door.

Over the cobbles he clatters and clangs in the dark inn-yard;
And he taps with his whip on the shutters, but all is locked and
　　barred;
He whistles a tune to the window, and who should be waiting there
But the landlord's black-eyed daughter,
　　Bess, the landlord's daughter,
Plaiting a dark red love-knot into her long black hair.

ALFRED NOYES

51　　　　　*The Rolling English Road*

BEFORE the Roman came to Rye or out to Severn strode,
The rolling English drunkard made the rolling English road.
A reeling road, a rolling road, that rambles round the shire,
And after him the parson ran, the sexton and the squire;
A merry road, a mazy road, and such as we did tread
The night we went to Birmingham by way of Beachy Head.

I knew no harm of Bonaparte and plenty of the Squire,
And for to fight the Frenchman I did not much desire;
But I did bash their baggonets because they came arrayed
To straighten out the crooked road an English drunkard
    made,
Where you and I went down the lane with ale-mugs in our
    hands,
The night we went to Glastonbury by way of Goodwin
    Sands.

His sins they were forgiven him; or why do flowers run
Behind him; and the hedges all strengthening in the sun?
The wild thing went from left to right and knew not which
    was which,
But the wild rose was above him when they found him in the
    ditch.
God pardon us, nor harden us; we did not see so clear
The night we went to Bannockburn by way of Brighton Pier.

My friends, we will not go again or ape an ancient rage,
Or stretch the folly of our youth to be the shame of age,
But walk with clearer eyes and ears this path that wandereth,
And see undrugged in evening light the decent inn of death;
For there is good news yet to hear and fine things to be seen,
Before we go to Paradise by way of Kensal Green.

G. K. CHESTERTON

By the old Moulmein Pagoda, lookin' lazy at the sea,
There's a Burma girl a-settin', and I know she thinks o' me;
For the wind is in the palm-trees, and the temple-bells they
    say:
'Come you back, you British soldier; come you back to
        Mandalay!'
    Come you back to Mandalay,
    Where the old Flotilla lay:
    Can't you 'ear their paddles chunkin' from Rangoon to
        Mandalay?
    On the road to Mandalay,
    Where the flyin'-fishes play,
    An' the dawn comes up like thunder outer China 'crost
        the Bay!

'Er petticoat was yaller an' 'er little cap was green,
An' 'er name was Supi-yaw-lat—jes' the same as Theebaw's
        Queen,
An' I seed her first a-smokin' of a whackin' white cheroot,
An' a-wastin' Christian kisses on an 'eathen idol's foot:
    Bloomin' idol made o' mud—
    Wot they called the Great Gawd Budd—
    Plucky lot she cared for idols when I kissed 'er where
        she stud!
    On the road to Mandalay . . .

When the mist was on the rice-fields an' the sun was
        droppin' slow,
She'd git 'er little banjo an' she'd sing '*Kulla-lo-lo!*'
With 'er arm upon my shoulder an' 'er cheek agin my cheek
We useter watch the steamers an' the *hathis* pilin' teak.

Elephints a-pilin' teak
In the sludgy, squdgy creek,
Where the silence 'ung that 'eavy you was 'arf afraid to
    speak!
On the road to Mandalay . . .

But that's all shove be'ind me—long ago an' fur away,
An' there ain't no 'buses runnin' from the Bank to Man-
    dalay;
An' I'm learnin' 'ere in London what the ten-year soldier
    tells:
'If you've 'eard the East a-callin', you won't never 'eed
    naught else.'
    No! you won't 'eed nothin' else
    But them spicy garlic smells,
    An' the sunshine an' the palm-trees an' the tinkly
        temple-bells;
    On the road to Mandalay . . .

I am sick o' wastin' leather on these gritty pavin'-stones,
An' the blasted English drizzle wakes the fever in my bones;
Tho' I walks with fifty 'ousemaids outer Chelsea to the
    Strand,
An' they talks a lot o' lovin', but wot do they understand?
    Beefy face an' grubby 'and—
    Law! wot do they understand?
    I've a neater, sweeter maiden in a cleaner, greener land!
    On the road to Mandalay . . .

Ship me somewheres east of Suez, where the best is like the
    worst,
Where there aren't no Ten Commandments an' a man can
    raise a thirst;

For the temple-bells are callin', an' it's there that I would
     be—
By the old Moulmein Pagoda, looking lazy at the sea;
    On the road to Mandalay,
    Where the old Flotilla lay,
    With our sick beneath the awnings when we went to
     Mandalay!
    On the road to Mandalay,
    Where the flyin'-fishes play,
    An' the dawn comes up like thunder outer China 'crost
     the Bay!

RUDYARD KIPLING

53 *The Way through the Woods*

THEY shut the road through the woods
Seventy years ago.
Weather and rain have undone it again,
And now you would never know
There was once a way through the woods
Before they planted the trees.
It is underneath the coppice and heath
And the thin anemones.
Only the keeper sees
That, where the ring-dove broods,
And the badgers roll at ease,
There was once a road through the woods.

Yet, if you enter the woods
Of a summer evening late,
When the night-air cools on the trout-ringed pools
Where the otter whistles his mate,
(They fear not men in the woods,

Because they see so few.)
You will hear the beat of a horse's feet,
And the swish of a skirt in the dew,
Steadily cantering through
The misty solitudes,
As though they perfectly knew
The old lost road through the woods. . . .
But there is no road through the woods.

RUDYARD KIPLING

54 *The Night-Piece: To Julia*

HER eyes the glow-worm lend thee,
The shooting stars attend thee;
    And the elves also,
    Whose little eyes glow
Like the sparks of fire, befriend thee.

No Will-o'-the-wisp mislight thee,
Nor snake or slow-worm bite thee;
    But on, on thy way
    Not making a stay,
Since ghost there's none to affright thee.

Let not the dark thee cumber:
What though the moon does slumber?
    The stars of the night
    Will lend thee their light
Like tapers clear without number.

Then, Julia, let me woo thee,
Thus, thus to come unto me;
    And when I shall meet
    Thy silv'ry feet,
My soul I'll pour into thee.

R. HERRICK

55 *Spring*

SPRING, the sweet Spring, is the year's pleasant king;
Then blooms each thing, then maids dance in a ring,
Cold doth not sting, the pretty birds do sing—
    Cuckoo, jug-jug, pu-we, to-witta-woo!

The palm and may make country houses gay,
Lambs frisk and play, the shepherds pipe all day,
And we hear aye birds tune this merry lay—
    Cuckoo, jug-jug, pu-we, to-witta-woo!

The fields breathe sweet, the daisies kiss our feet,
Young lovers meet, old wives a-sunning sit,
In every street these tunes our ears do greet—
    Cuckoo, jug-jug, pu-we, to-witta-woo!
    Spring, the sweet Spring!

T. NASHE

56 *The Fifteen Acres*

I

I CLING and swing
    On a branch, or sing
Through the cool, clear hush of morning, O!

Or fling my wing
On the air, and bring
To sleepier birds a warning, O!

That the night's in flight,
And the sun's in sight,
And the dew is the grass adorning, O!

And the green leaves swing
As I sing, sing, sing,
Up by the river,
Down by the dell,
To the little wee nest
Where the big tree fell,
So early in the morning, O!

II

I flit and twit
In the sun for a bit
When his light so bright is shining, O!

Or sit and fit
My plumes, or knit
Straw plaits for the nest's nice lining, O!

And she with glee,
Shows unto me,
Under her wings reclining, O!

And I sing that Peg
Has an egg, egg, egg!
Up by the oat-field,
Round the mill;
Past the meadow,
Down the hill,
So early in the morning, O!

III

I stoop and swoop
On the air, or loop
Through the trees, and then go soaring, O!

To group, with a troop
On the skiey poop
While the sun behind is roaring, O!

I skim and swim
By the cloud's red rim;
And up to the azure flooring, O!

And my wide wings drip,
As I slip, slip, slip,
   Down through the raindrops,
      Back where Peg
   Broods in the nest
      On the little white egg
   So early in the morning, O!

JAMES STEPHENS

57

The Twa Corbies

As I was walking all alane
I heard twa corbies making a mane:
The tane unto the tither did say,
'Whar sall we gang and dine the day?'

'—In behint yon auld fail dyke
I wot there lies a new-slain knight;
And naebody kens that he lies there
But his hawk, his hound, and his lady fair.

corbies, ravens.   *fail*, turf.

'His hound is to the hunting gane,
  His hawk to fetch the wild-fowl hame,
  His lady's ta'en anither mate,
  So we may mak our dinner sweet.

'Ye'll sit on his white hause-bane,
  And I'll pike out his bonny blue e'en:
  Wi' ae lock o' his gowden hair
  We'll theek our nest when it grows bare.

'Mony a one for him maks mane,
  But nane sall ken whar he is gane:
  O'er his white banes, when they are bare,
  The wind sall blaw for evermair.'

BALLAD

hause-bane, neckbone.   *theek*, thatch.

58   *To the Cuckoo*

O BLITHE new-comer! I have heard,
  I hear thee and rejoice.
O cuckoo! shall I call thee bird,
  Or but a wandering voice?

While I am lying on the grass
  Thy twofold shout I hear;
From hill to hill it seems to pass,
  At once far off, and near.

Though babbling only to the Vale,
  Of sunshine and of flowers,
Thou bringest unto me a tale
  Of visionary hours.

Thrice welcome, darling of the Spring!
  Even yet thou art to me
No bird, but an invisible thing,
  A voice, a mystery.

The same whom in my schoolboy days
  I listened to; that Cry
Which made me look a thousand ways
  In bush, and tree, and sky.

To seek thee did I often rove
  Through woods and on the green;
And thou wert still a hope, a love;
  Still longed for, never seen.

And I can listen to thee yet;
  Can lie upon the plain
And listen, till I do beget
  That golden time again.

O blessèd bird! the earth we pace
  Again appears to be
An unsubstantial, faery place;
  That is fit home for Thee.

W. WORDSWORTH

59 *The Kingfisher*

IT was the Rainbow gave thee birth,
  And left thee all her lovely hues;
And, as her mother's name was Tears,
  So runs it in my blood to choose
For haunts the lonely pools, and keep
In company with trees that weep.

Go you and, with such glorious hues,
  Live with proud peacocks in green parks;
On lawns as smooth as shining glass,
Let every feather show its marks;
Get thee on boughs and clap thy wings
Before the windows of proud kings.

Nay, lovely Bird, thou art not vain;
  Thou hast no proud, ambitious mind;
I also love a quiet place
  That's green, away from all mankind;
A lonely pool, and let a tree
Sigh with her bosom over me.

W. H. DAVIES

60 *The Wild Duck*

TWILIGHT. Red in the west.
Dimness. A glow on the wood.
The teams plod home to rest.
The wild duck come to glean.
O souls not understood,
What a wild cry in the pool;
What things have the farm ducks seen
That they cry so—huddle and cry?

Only the soul that goes.
Eager. Eager. Flying.
Over the globe of the moon,
Over the wood that glows.
Wings linked. Necks a-strain,
A rush and a wild crying.

.   .   .   .   .

A cry of the long pain
In the reeds of a steel lagoon,
In a land that no man knows.

JOHN MASEFIELD

61   *Stage Directions*

TRUMPETS. Enter a King, in the sunset glare.
He sits in an antique chair. He fingers an antique ring.
The heavy cloak on his back is gold and black.

The hall is tall with gloom. A window stands
Full of scarlet sky. The hands of trees entreat the room,
Plucking and plucking the pane. An oblong stain

Of scarlet is flat on the floor. The projected flare
Slants to the foot of the chair. The chamber's farther door
Slowly advances its edge. A smoky wedge

Of thick blue mist, growing wider as the door swings
Noiseless, twitches the King's hands. He is crouched like a
    spider.
His eyes are green as glass. Shudderings pass

That shrink him deep in his cloak. The door is wide.
The doorway, from side to side, is packed with mist like
    smoke.
The dreadful scarlet dies from the windowed skies.

Silence crosses the room. Nothing more.
Silence crowds from the door, gathers, gathers in gloom.
His fluttering fingers rise to cover his eyes.

Silence says nothing at all. It is thickly pressed,
Like a multitude obsessed with terror from wall to wall.
Silence, deep with dread, is the weight of lead

That slowly constricts his breast. Fingers fight
At the throat, in fierce despite of death, as the drowned resist
Green gulfs that roar and ring. . . . Exit the King.

W. R. BENET

62   *Henry V before Harfleur*

ONCE more unto the breach, dear friends, once more;
Or close the wall up with our English dead!
In peace there's nothing so becomes a man
As modest stillness and humility:
But when the blast of war blows in our ears,
Then imitate the action of the tiger;
Stiffen the sinews, summon up the blood,
Disguise fair nature with hard-favour'd rage;
Then lend the eye a terrible aspect;
Let it pry through the portage of the head
Like the brass cannon; let the brow o'erwhelm it
As fearfully as doth a galled rock
O'erhang and jutty his confounded base,
Swill'd with the wild and wasteful ocean.
Now set the teeth, and stretch the nostril wide;
Hold hard the breath, and bend up every spirit
To his full height!—On, on, you noblest English,
Whose blood is fet from fathers of war-proof!—
Fathers that, like so many Alexanders,
Have in these parts from morn till even fought,
And sheath'd their swords for lack of argument:—
Dishonour not your mothers; now attest

That those whom you call'd fathers did beget you!
Be copy now to men of grosser blood,
And teach them how to war!—And you, good yeomen,
Whose limbs were made in England, show us here
The mettle of your pasture; let us swear
That you are worthy of your breeding: which I doubt not;
For there is none of you so mean and base,
That hath not noble lustre in your eyes.
I see you stand like greyhounds in the slips,
Straining upon the start. The game's afoot:
Follow your spirit; and upon this charge
Cry 'God for Harry, England, and St. George!'

W. SHAKESPEARE

63   *The War Song of Dinas Vawr*

THE mountain sheep are sweeter,
But the valley sheep are fatter;
We therefore deemed it meeter
To carry off the latter.
We made an expedition;
We met a host, and quelled it;
We forced a strong position,
And killed the men who held it.

On Dyfed's richest valley,
Where herds of kine were browsing,
We made a mighty sally,
To furnish our carousing.
Fierce warriors rushed to meet us;
We met them, and o'erthrew them:
They struggled hard to beat us;
But we conquered them, and slew them.

131

As we drove our prize at leisure,
The king marched forth to catch us:
His rage surpassed all measure,
But his people could not match us.
He fled to his hall-pillars;
And, ere our force we led off,
Some sacked his house and cellars,
While others cut his head off.

We there, in strife bewildering,
Spilt blood enough to swim in:
We orphaned many children,
And widowed many women.
The eagles and the ravens
We glutted with our foemen;
The heroes and the cravens,
The spearmen and the bowmen.

We brought away from battle,
And much their land bemoaned them,
Two thousand head of cattle,
And the head of him who owned them:
Ednyfed, King of Dyfed,
His head was borne before us;
His wine and beasts supplied our feasts,
And his overthrow, our chorus.

T. L. PEACOCK

WE are they who come faster than fate: we are they who
    ride early or late:
We storm at your ivory gate: Pale Kings of the Sunset,
    beware!
Not on silk nor in samet we lie, not in curtained solemnity
    die
Among women who chatter and cry, and children who
    mumble a prayer.
But we sleep by the ropes of the camp, and we rise with a
    shout, and we tramp
With the sun or the moon for a lamp, and the spray of the
    wind in our hair.

From the lands, where the elephants are, to the forts of
    Merou and Balghar,
Our steel we have brought and our star to shine on the
    ruins of Rum.
We have marched from the Indus to Spain, and by God we
    will go there again;
We have stood on the shore of the plain where the Waters of
    Destiny boom.
A mart of destruction we made at Jalula where men were
    afraid,
For death was a difficult trade, and the sword was a broker
    of doom;

And the Spear was a Desert Physician who cured not a few
    of ambition,
And drave not a few to perdition with medicine bitter and
    strong:
And the shield was a grief to the fool and as bright as a
    desolate pool,

And as straight as the rock of Stamboul when their cavalry
    thundered along:
For the coward was drowned with the brave when our battle
    sheered up like a wave,
And the dead to the desert we gave, and the glory to God in
    our song.

J. E. FLECKER

65   *The Song of the Ungirt Runners*

WE swing ungirded hips,
And lightened are our eyes,
The rain is on our lips,
We do not run for prize.
We know not whom we trust
Nor whitherward we fare,
But we run because we must
   Through the great wide air.

The waters of the seas
Are troubled as by storm.
The tempest strips the trees
And does not leave them warm.
Does the tearing tempest pause?
Do the tree-tops ask it why?
So we run without a cause
   'Neath the big bare sky.

The rain is on our lips,
We do not run for prize.
But the storm the water whips
And the wave howls to the skies.

The winds arise and strike it
And scatter it like sand,
And we run because we like it
Through the broad bright land.
                    C. H. SORLEY

Boots

WE'RE foot—slog—slog—slog—sloggin' over Africa—
Foot—foot—foot—foot—sloggin' over Africa—
(Boots—boots—boots—boots—movin' up and down again!)
     There's no discharge in the war!

Seven—six—eleven—five—nine-an'-twenty mile to-day—
Four—eleven—seventeen—thirty-two the day before—
(Boots—boots—boots—boots—movin' up and down again!)
     There's no discharge in the war!

Don't—don't—don't—don't—look at what's in front of you.
(Boots—boots—boots—boots—movin' up an' down again);
Men—men—men—men—men go mad with watchin' 'em,
     An' there's no discharge in the war!

Try—try—try—try—to think o' something different—
Oh—my—God—keep—me from goin' lunatic!
(Boots—boots—boots—boots—movin' up an' down again!)
     There's no discharge in the war!

Count—count—count—count—the bullets in the bandoliers.
If—your—eyes—drop—they will get atop o' you!
(Boots—boots—boots—boots—movin' up and down again) -
     There's no discharge in the war!

f We—can—stick—out—'unger, thirst, an' weariness,
But—not—not—not—not the chronic sight of 'em—
Boots—boots—boots—boots—movin' up an' down again,
    An' there's no discharge in the war!

'Tain't—so—bad—by—day because o' company,
But night—brings—long—strings—o' forty thousand million
Boots—boots—boots—boots—movin' up an' down again,
    There's no discharge in the war!

I—'ave—marched—six—weeks in 'Ell an' certify
It—is—not—fire—devils, dark, or anything,
But boots—boots—boots—boots—movin' up an' down again,
    An' there's no discharge in the war!

RUDYARD KIPLING

67   *Tarantella*

Do you remember an Inn,
Miranda?
Do you remember an Inn?
And the tedding and the spreading
Of the straw for a bedding,
And the fleas that tease in the High Pyrenees,
And the wine that tasted of the tar,
And the cheers and the jeers of the young muleteers
(Under the vine of the dark verandah)?
Do you remember an Inn, Miranda,
Do you remember an Inn?
And the cheers and the jeers of the young muleteers
Who hadn't got a penny,
And who weren't paying any,
And the hammer at the doors and the Din?

And the Hip! Hop! Hap!
Of the clap
Of the hands to the twirl and the swirl
Of the girl gone chancing,
Glancing,
Dancing,
Backing and advancing,
Snapping of the clapper to the spin
Out and in——
And the Ting, Tong, Tang of the Guitar!
Do you remember an Inn,
Miranda?
Do you remember an Inn?

Never more,
Miranda,
Never more.
Only the high peaks hoar:
And Aragon a torrent at the door.
No sound
In the walls of the Halls where falls
The tread
Of the feet of the dead to the ground,
No sound:
But the boom
Of the far Waterfall like Doom.

HILAIRE BELLOC

68 *Mountain Lion*

CLIMBING through the January snow, into the Lobo
    Canyon
Dark grow the spruce-trees, blue is the balsam, water
    sounds still unfrozen, and the trail is still evident.

Men!
Two men!
Men! The only animal in the world to fear!

They hesitate.
We hesitate.
They have a gun.
We have no gun.

Then we all advance, to meet.

Two Mexicans, strangers, emerging out of the dark and
    snow and inwardness of the Lobo valley.
What are you doing here on this vanishing trail?

What is he carrying?
Something yellow.
A deer?

Qué tiene, amigo?
León—

He smiles, foolishly, as if he were caught doing wrong.
And we smile, foolishly, as if we didn't know.
He is quite gentle and dark-faced.

It is a mountain lion,
A long, long slim cat, yellow like a lioness.
Dead.

He trapped her this morning, he says, smiling foolishly.

Lift up her face,
Her round, bright face, bright as frost.
Her round, fine-fashioned head, with two dead ears;

And stripes in the brilliant frost of her face, sharp, fine dark
    rays,
Dark, keen, fine eyes in the brilliant frost of her face.
Beautiful dead eyes.

Hermoso es!

They go out towards the open;
We go on into the gloom of Lobo.
And above the trees I found her lair,
A hole in the blood-orange brilliant rocks that stick up, a
    little cave.
And bones, and twigs, and a perilous ascent.

So, she will never leap up that way again, with the yellow
    flash of a mountain lion's long shoot!
And her bright striped frost-face will never watch any more,
    out of the shadow of the cave in the blood-orange rock,
Above the trees of the Lobo dark valley-mouth!

Instead, I look out.
And out to the dim of the desert, like a dream, never real;
To the snow of the Sangre de Cristo mountains, the ice of
    the mountains of Picoris,
And near across at the opposite steep of snow, green trees
    motionless standing in snow, like a Christmas toy.

And I think in this empty world there was room for me and a
    mountain lion.
And I think in the world beyond, how easily we might spare
    a million or two of humans
And never miss them.
Yet what a gap in the world, the missing white frost-face
    of that slim yellow mountain lion!

D. H. LAWRENCE

THERE was a Boy, whose name was Jim;
His Friends were very good to him.
They gave him Tea, and Cakes, and Jam,
And slices of delicious Ham,
And Chocolate with pink inside,
And little Tricycles to ride,
And read him Stories through and through,
And even took him to the Zoo—
And there it was the dreadful Fate
Befel him, which I now relate.

You know—at least you *ought* to know,
For I have often told you so—
That Children never are allowed
To leave their Nurses in a Crowd;
Now this was Jim's especial Foible,
He ran away when he was able,
And on this inauspicious day
He slipped his hand and ran away!
He hadn't gone a yard when—Bang!
With open Jaws, a Lion sprang,
And hungrily began to eat
The Boy; beginning at his feet.

Now, just imagine how it feels
When first your toes, and then your heels,
And then by gradual degrees,
Your shins and ankles, calves and knees,
Are slowly eaten, bit by bit.
No wonder Jim detested it!
No wonder that he shouted 'Hi!'
The Honest Keeper heard his cry,

Though very fat he almost ran
To help the little gentleman.
'Ponto!' he ordered as he came
(For Ponto was the Lion's name),
'Ponto!' he cried, with angry Frown,
'Let go, Sir! Down, Sir! Put it down!'

The Lion made a sudden Stop,
He let the Dainty Morsel drop,
And slunk reluctant to his Cage,
Snarling with Disappointed Rage.
But when he bent him over Jim,
The Honest Keeper's Eyes were dim.
The Lion having reached his Head,
The Miserable Boy was dead!

When Nurse informed his Parents, they
Were more Concerned than I can say:—
His Mother, as she dried her eyes,
Said, 'Well—it gives me no surprise,
He would not do as he was told!'
His Father, who was self-controlled,
Bade all the children round attend
To James' miserable end,
And always keep a-hold of Nurse
For fear of finding something worse.

HILAIRE BELLOC

On a Favourite Cat, drowned in a Tub of Goldfishes

'TWAS on a lofty vase's side,
Where China's gayest art had dyed
  The azure flowers that blow;
Demurest of the tabby kind,
The pensive Selima reclined,
  Gazed on the lake below.

Her conscious tail her joy declared;
The fair round face, the snowy beard,
  The velvet of her paws,
Her coat that with the tortoise vies,
Her ears of jet, and emerald eyes,
  She saw; and purr'd applause.

Still had she gazed; but 'midst the tide
Two angel forms were seen to glide,
  The Genii of the stream:
Their scaly armour's Tyrian hue
Thro' richest purple to the view
  Betray'd a golden gleam.

The hapless Nymph with wonder saw:
A whisker first and then a claw,
  With many an ardent wish,
She stretch'd in vain, to reach the prize.
What female heart can gold despise?
  What Cat's averse to fish?

Presumptuous Maid! with looks intent
Again she stretch'd, again she bent,
  Nor knew the gulf between.

(Malignant Fate sat by, and smiled)
The slipp'ry verge her feet beguiled,
    She tumbled headlong in!

Eight times emerging from the flood
She mew'd to ev'ry watery god,
    Some speedy aid to send.
No Dolphin came, no Nereid stirr'd;
Nor cruel Tom nor Susan heard.
    A fav'rite has no friend!

From hence, ye Beauties, undeceived,
Know, one false step is ne'er retrieved,
    And be with caution bold;
Not all that tempts your wand'ring eyes
And heedless hearts, is lawful prize;
    Nor all that glisters, gold.

                                    T. GRAY

71   *To a Mouse*

On turning her up in her nest with the plough, November 1785

WEE, sleekit, cow'rin', tim'rous beastie,
O what a panic's in thy breastie!
Thou need na start awa sae hasty,
    Wi' bickering brattle!
I wad be laith to rin an' chase thee
    Wi' murd'ring pattle!

I'm truly sorry Man's dominion
Has broken Nature's social union,

bickering brattle, hurried scamper.   *pattle*, plough-staff.

143

An' justifies that ill opinion,
   Which makes thee startle,
At me, thy poor, earth-born companion,
   An' fellow-mortal!

I doubt na, whiles, but thou may thieve;
What then? poor beastie, thou maun live!
A daimen-icker in a thrave
     'S a sma' request:
I'll get a blessin' wi' the lave,
     And never miss't!

Thy wee-bit housie, too, in ruin!
Its silly wa's the win's are strewin'!
An' naething, now, to big a new ane,
     O' foggage green!
An' bleak December's winds ensuin',
     Baith snell an' keen!

Thou saw the fields laid bare and waste,
An' weary winter comin' fast,
An' cozie here, beneath the blast,
     Thou thought to dwell,
Till crash! the cruel coulter past
     Out thro' thy cell.

That wee-bit heap o' leaves and stibble
Has cost thee mony a weary nibble!
Now thou's turn'd out, for a' thy trouble,
     But house or hald,
To thole the Winter's sleety dribble,
     An' cranreuch cauld!

daimen-icker, occasional ear.   *thrave*, twenty-four sheaves.   *lave*, rest.
big, build.   *snell*, bitter.   *thole*, endure.   *cranreuch*, hoar-frost.

But, Mousie, thou art no thy lane,
In proving foresight may be vain:
The best laid schemes o' Mice an' Men
      Gang aft a-gley,
An' lea'e us nought but grief an' pain
      For promis'd joy.

Still thou art blest compar'd wi' me!
The present only toucheth thee:
But Och! I backward cast my e'e
      On prospects drear!
An' forward tho' I canna see,
      I guess an' fear!

ROBERT BURNS

thy lane, alone.   *a-gley*, awry.

72   *All but Blind*

ALL but blind
  In his chambered hole
Gropes for worms
  The four-clawed Mole.

All but blind
  In the evening sky
The hooded Bat
  Twirls softly by.

All but blind
  In the burning day
The Barn-Owl blunders
  On her way.

And blind as are
 These three to me,
So, blind to Some-One
 I must be.
WALTER DE LA MARE

73   *The Tiger*

TIGER, tiger, burning bright
In the forests of the night,
What immortal hand or eye
Could frame thy fearful symmetry?

In what distant deeps or skies
Burned the fire of thine eyes?
On what wings dare he aspire?
What the hand dare seize the fire?

And what shoulder and what art
Could twist the sinews of thy heart?
And, when thy heart began to beat,
What dread hand and what dread feet?

What the hammer? What the chain?
In what furnace was thy brain?
What the anvil? What dread grasp
Dare it's deadly terrors clasp?

When the stars threw down their spears,
And water'd heaven with their tears,
Did He smile His work to see?
Did He who made the lamb make thee?
WILLIAM BLAKE

Jabberwocky

'Twas brillig, and the slithy toves
    Did gyre and gimble in the wabe;
All mimsy were the borogroves,
    And the mome raths outgrabe.

'Beware the Jabberwock, my son!
    The jaws that bite, the claws that catch!
Beware the Jubjub bird, and shun
    The frumious Bandersnatch!'

He took his vorpal sword in hand:
    Long time the manxome foe he sought—
So rested he by the Tumtum tree,
    And stood awhile in thought.

And, as in uffish thought he stood,
    The Jabberwock, with eyes of flame,
Came whiffling through the tulgy wood,
    And burbled as it came!

One, two! One, two! And through and through
    The vorpal blade went snicker-snack!
He left it dead, and with its head
    He went galumphing back.

'And hast thou slain the Jabberwock?
    Come to my arms, my beamish boy!
O frabjous day! Callooh! Callay!'
    He chortled in his joy.

'Twas brillig, and the slithy toves
    Did gyre and gimble in the wabe:
All mimsy were the borogroves,
    And the mome raths outgrabe.

LEWIS CARROLL

'YOU are old, Father William,' the young man said,
  'And your hair has become very white;
And yet you incessantly stand on your head—
  Do you think, at your age, it is right?'

'In my youth,' Father William replied to his son,
  'I feared it might injure the brain;
But now that I'm perfectly sure I have none,
  Why, I do it again and again.'

'You are old,' said the youth, 'as I mentioned before,
  And have grown most uncommonly fat;
Yet you turned a back-somersault in at the door—
  Pray, what is the reason of that?'

'In my youth,' said the sage, as he shook his grey locks,
  'I kept all my limbs very supple
By the use of this ointment—one shilling the box—
  Allow me to sell you a couple.'

'You are old,' said the youth, 'and your jaws are too weak
  For anything tougher than suet;
Yet you finished the goose, with the bones and the beak—
  Pray, how did you manage to do it?'

'In my youth,' said his father, 'I took to the law,
  And argued each case with my wife;
And the muscular strength which it gave to my jaw
  Has lasted the rest of my life.'

'You are old,' said the youth; 'one would hardly suppose
    That your eye was as steady as ever;
Yet you balanced an eel on the end of your nose—
    What made you so awfully clever?'

'I have answered three questions, and that is enough,'
    Said his father; 'don't give yourself airs!
Do you think I can listen all day to such stuff?
    Be off, or I'll kick you down stairs!'

LEWIS CARROLL

76   *Gunga Din*

YOU may talk o' gin and beer
When you're quartered safe out 'ere,
An' you're sent to penny-fights an' Aldershot it;
But when it comes to slaughter
You will do your work on water,
An' you'll lick the bloomin' boots of 'im that's got it.
Now in Injia's sunny clime,
Where I used to spend my time,
A-servin' of 'Er Majesty the Queen,
Of all them blackfaced crew
The finest man I knew
Was our regimental bhisti, Gunga Din,
        He was 'Din! Din! Din!
    'You limpin' lump o' brick-dust, Gunga Din!
        'Hi! Slippy *hitherao*!
        'Water, get it! *Panee lao*,
    'You squidgy-nosed old idol, Gunga Din.'

149

The uniform 'e wore
Was nothin' much before,
An' rather less than 'arf o' that be'ind,
For a piece o' twisty rag
An' a goatskin water-bag
Was all the field-equipment e' could find.
When the sweatin' troop-train lay
In a sidin' through the day,
Where the 'eat would make your bloomin' eyebrows crawl,
We shouted 'Harry By!'
Till our throats were bricky-dry,
Then we wopped 'im 'cause 'e couldn't serve us all.
    It was 'Din! Din! Din!
  'You 'eathen, where the mischief 'ave you been?
    'You put some *juldee* in it
    'Or I'll *marrow* you this minute
  'If you don't fill up my helmet, Gunga Din!'

'E would dot an' carry one
Till the longest day was done;
An' 'e didn't seem to know the use o' fear.
If we charged or broke or cut,
You could bet your bloomin' nut,
'E'd be waitin' fifty paces right flank rear.
With 'is mussick on 'is back,
'E would skip with our attack,
An' watch us till the bugles made, 'Retire,'
An' for all 'is dirty 'ide
'E was white, clear white, inside
When 'e went to tend the wounded under fire!
    It was 'Din! Din! Din!'
  With the bullets kickin' dust-spots on the green,

When the cartridges ran out,
  You could hear the front-ranks shout,
'Hi! ammunition-mules an' Gunga Din!'

I shan't forgit the night
When I dropped be'ind the fight
With a bullet where my belt-plate should 'a' been.
I was chokin' mad with thirst,
An' the man that spied me first
Was our good old grinnin', gruntin' Gunga Din.
'E lifted up my 'ead,
An' he plugged me where I bled,
An' 'e guv me 'arf-a-pint o' water green.
It was crawlin' and it stunk,
But of all the drinks I've drunk,
I'm gratefullest to one from Gunga Din.
    It was 'Din! Din! Din!
  "Ere's a beggar with a bullet through 'is spleen;
   "E's chawin' up the ground,
    'An' 'e's kickin' all around:
  'For Gawd's sake git the water, Gunga Din!'

'E carried me away
To where a dooli lay,
An' a bullet come an' drilled the beggar clean.
'E put me safe inside,
An' just before 'e died,
'I 'ope you liked your drink,' sez Gunga Din.
So I'll meet 'im later on
At the place where 'e is gone—
Where it's always double drill and no canteen.
'E'll be squattin' on the coals
Givin' drink to poor damned souls,
An' I'll get a swig in hell from Gunga Din!

151

Yes, Din! Din! Din!
You Lazarushian-leather Gunga Din!
  Though I've belted you and flayed you,
  By the livin' Gawd that made you,
You're a better man than I am, Gunga Din!

RUDYARD KIPLING

77   *Shameful Death*

THERE were four of us about that bed;
  The mass-priest knelt at the side,
I and his mother stood at the head,
  Over his feet lay the bride;
We were quite sure that he was dead,
  Though his eyes were open wide.

He did not die in the night,
  He did not die in the day,
But in the morning twilight
  His spirit pass'd away,
When neither sun nor moon was bright,
  And the trees were merely grey.

He was not slain with the sword,
  Knight's axe, or the knightly spear,
Yet spoke he never a word
  After he came in here;
I cut away the cord
  From the neck of my brother dear.

He did not strike one blow,
  For the recreants came behind,
In a place where the hornbeams grow,
  A path right hard to find,
For the hornbeam boughs swing so,
  That the twilight makes it blind.

They lighted a great torch then,
  When his arms were pinion'd fast,
Sir John the knight of the Fen,
  Sir Guy of the Dolorous Blast,
With knights threescore and ten,
  Hung brave Lord Hugh at last.

I am threescore and ten,
  And my hair is all turn'd grey,
But I met Sir John of the Fen
  Long ago on a summer day,
And am glad to think of the moment when
  I took his life away.

I am threescore and ten,
  And my strength is mostly pass'd,
But long ago I and my men,
  When the sky was overcast,
And the smoke roll'd over the reeds of the fen,
  Slew Guy of the Dolorous Blast.

And now, knights all of you,
I pray you pray for Sir Hugh,
A good knight and a true,
And for Alice, his wife, pray too.

WILLIAM MORRIS

AND the first grey of morning fill'd the east.
And the fog rose out of the Oxus stream.
But all the Tartar camp along the stream
Was hush'd, and still the men were plunged in sleep:
Sohrab alone, he slept not: all night long
He had lain wakeful, tossing on his bed;
But when the grey dawn stole into his tent,
He rose, and clad himself, and girt his sword,
And took his horseman's cloak, and left his tent,
And went abroad into the cold wet fog,
Through the dim camp, to Peran-Wisa's tent.

   .   .   .   .

And Peran-Wisa heard him, though the step
Was dull'd; for he slept light, an old man's sleep;
And he rose quickly on one arm, and said:—
   'Who art thou? for it is not yet clear dawn.
Speak! is there news, or any night alarm?'
   But Sohrab came to the bedside, and said: —
'Thou know'st me, Peran-Wisa: it is I.
The sun is not yet risen, and the foe
Sleep; but I sleep not; all night long I lie
Tossing and wakeful, and I come to thee.
For so did King Afrasiab bid me seek
Thy counsel, and to heed thee as thy son,
In Samarcand, before the army march'd;
And I will tell thee what my heart desires.
Thou know'st if, since from Ader-baijan first
I came among the Tartars, and bore arms,
I have still served Afrasiab well, and shown,
At my boy's years, the courage of a man.
This too thou know'st, that, while I still bear on
The conquering Tartar ensigns through the world,

And beat the Persians back on every field,
I seek one man, one man, and one alone—
Rustum, my father; who, I hop'd, should greet,
Should one day greet, upon some well-fought field,
His not unworthy, not inglorious son.
So I long hop'd, but him I never find.
Come then, hear now, and grant me what I ask.
Let the two armies rest to-day; but I
Will challenge forth the bravest Persian lords
To meet me, man to man: if I prevail,
Rustum will surely hear it; if I fall—
Old man, the dead need no one, claim no kin.
Dim is the rumour of a common fight,
Where host meets host, and many names are sunk:
But of a single combat Fame speaks clear.'

    He spoke: and Peran-Wisa took the hand
Of the young man in his, and sigh'd, and said:—
    O Sohrab, an unquiet heart is thine!
Canst thou not rest among the Tartar chiefs,
And share the battle's common chance with us
Who love thee, but must press for ever first,
In single fight incurring single risk,
To find a father thou hast never seen?
That were far best, my son, to stay with us
Unmurmuring; in our tents, while it is war,
And when 'tis truce, then in Afrasiab's towns.
But, if this one desire indeed rules all,
To seek out Rustum—seek him not through fight:
Seek him in peace, and carry to his arms,
O Sohrab, carry an unwounded son!

   ·   ·   ·   ·   ·   ·

Then Peran-Wisa with his herald came
Threading the Tartar squadrons to the front,
And with his staff kept back the foremost ranks.

And when Ferood, who led the Persians, saw
That Peran-Wisa kept the Tartars back,
He took his spear, and to the front he came,
And check'd his ranks, and fix'd them where they stood.
And the old Tartar came upon the sand
Betwixt the silent hosts, and spake, and said:—
    'Ferood, and ye, Persians and Tartars, hear!
Let there be truce between the hosts to-day.
But choose a champion from the Persian lords
To fight our champion, Sohrab, man to man.'

So spake he; and Ferood stood forth and said:—
'Old man, be it agreed as thou hast said.
Let Sohrab arm, and we will find a man.'
    He spoke; and Peran-Wisa turn'd and strode
Back through the opening squadrons to his tent.
But through the anxious Persians Gudurz ran,
And cross'd the camp which lay behind, and reach'd,
Out on the sands beyond it, Rustum's tents.
Of scarlet cloth they were, and glittering gay,
Just pitch'd: the high pavilion in the midst
Was Rustum's, and his men lay camp'd around.

    But Gudurz stood in the tent door and said:—
'The armies are drawn out, and stand at gaze:
For from the Tartars is a challenge brought
To pick a champion from the Persian lords
To fight their champion—and thou know'st his name—
Sohrab men call him, but his birth is hid.
O Rustum, like thy might is this young man's!
He has the wild stag's foot, the lion's heart.
And he is young, and Iran's Chiefs are old,
Or else too weak; and all eyes turn to thee.
Come down and help us, Rustum, or we lose.'

He spoke; but Rustum answer'd with a smile:—
'Go to! if Iran's Chiefs are old, then I
Am older: if the young are weak, the King
Errs strangely; for the King, for Kai-Khosroo,
Himself is young, and honours younger men,
And lets the agèd moulder to their graves.
Rustum he loves no more, but loves the young—
The young may rise at Sohrab's vaunts, not I.
For what care I, though all speak Sohrab's fame?
For would that I myself had such a son,
And not that one slight helpless girl I have,
A son so fam'd, so brave, to send to war.'

    He spoke, and smil'd; and Gudurz made reply:—
'What then, O Rustum, will men say to this,
When Sohrab dares our bravest forth, and seeks
Thee most of all, and thou, whom most he seeks,
Hidest thy face? Take heed lest men should say,
Like some old miser, Rustum hoards his fame,
And shuns to peril it with younger men.'

    And, greatly mov'd, then Rustum made reply:—
'O Gudurz, wherefore dost thou say such words?
Thou knowest better words than this to say.
What is one more, one less, obscure or fam'd,
Valiant or craven, young or old, to me?
Are not they mortal, am not I myself?
But who for men of naught would do great deeds?
Come, thou shalt see how Rustum hoards his fame.
But I will fight unknown, and in plain arms;
Let not men say of Rustum, he was match'd
In single fight with any mortal man.'

    He spake, and frown'd; and Gudurz turn'd, and ran
Back quickly through the camp in fear and joy,
Fear at his wrath, but joy that Rustum came.
But Rustum strode to his tent door, and call'd

His followers in, and bade them bring his arms,
And clad himself in steel: the arms he chose
Were plain, and on his shield was no device,
Only his helm was rich, inlaid with gold,
And from the fluted spine atop a plume
Of horsehair wav'd, a scarlet horsehair plume.
So arm'd, he issued forth; and Ruksh, his horse,
Follow'd him, like a faithful hound, at heel—
Ruksh, whose renown was nois'd through all the earth;
The horse, whom Rustum on a foray once
Did in Bokhara by the river find
A colt beneath its dam, and drove him home,
And rear'd him; a bright bay, with lofty crest;
Dight with a saddle-cloth of broider'd green
Crusted with gold, and on the ground were work'd
All beasts of chase, all beasts which hunters know:
So follow'd, Rustum left his tents, and cross'd
The camp, and to the Persian host appear'd.
And all the Persians knew him, and with shouts
Hail'd; but the Tartars knew not who he was.
And dear as the wet diver to the eyes
Of his pale wife who waits and weeps on shore,
By sandy Bahrein, in the Persian Gulf,
Plunging all day in the blue waves, at night,
Having made up his tale of precious pearls,
Rejoins her in their hut upon the sands—
So dear to the pale Persians Rustum came.

        And Rustum to the Persian front advanc'd,
And Sohrab arm'd in Haman's tent, and came.
And as afield the reapers cut a swathe
Down through the middle of a rich man's corn,
And on each side are squares of standing corn,
And in the midst a stubble, short and bare;
So on each side were squares of men, with spears

Bristling, and in the midst, the open sand.
And Rustum came upon the sand, and cast
His eyes towards the Tartar tents, and saw
Sohrab come forth, and ey'd him as he came.

As some rich woman, on a winter's morn,
Eyes through her silken curtains the poor drudge
Who with numb blacken'd fingers makes her fire—
At cock-crow, on a starlit winter's morn,
When the frost flowers the whiten'd window panes—
And wonders how she lives, and what the thoughts
Of that poor drudge may be; so Rustum ey'd
The unknown adventurous Youth, who from afar
Came seeking Rustum, and defying forth
All the most valiant chiefs: long he perus'd
His spirited air, and wonder'd who he was.
For very young he seem'd, tenderly rear'd;
Like some young cypress, tall, and dark, and straight,
Which in a queen's secluded garden throws
Its slight dark shadow on the moonlit turf,
By midnight, to a bubbling fountain's sound—
So slender Sohrab seem'd, so softly rear'd.
And a deep pity enter'd Rustum's soul
As he beheld him coming; and he stood,
And beckon'd to him with his hand, and said:—

'Oh thou young man, the air of Heaven is soft,
And warm, and pleasant; but the grave is cold.
Heaven's air is better than the cold dead grave.
Behold me: I am vast, and clad in iron,
And tried; and I have stood on many a field
Of blood, and I have fought with many a foe:
Never was that field lost, or that foe sav'd.
O Sohrab, wherefore wilt thou rush on death?
Be govern'd: quit the Tartar host, and come
To Iran, and be as my son to me,

And fight beneath my banner till I die.
There are no youths in Iran brave as thou.'
    So he spake, mildly: Sohrab heard his voice,
The mighty voice of Rustum; and he saw
His giant figure planted on the sand,
Sole, like some single tower, which a chief
Has builded on the waste in former years
Against the robbers; and he saw that head,
Streak'd with its first grey hairs: hope fill'd his soul;
And he ran forward and embrac'd his knees,
And clasp'd his hand within his own, and said:—
    'Oh, by thy father's head! by thine own soul!
Art thou not Rustum? speak! art thou not he?'
    But Rustum ey'd askance the kneeling youth,
And turned away, and spoke to his own soul:—
    'Ah me, I muse what this young fox may mean!
False, wily, boastful, are these Tartar boys.
For if I now confess this thing he asks,
And hide it not, but say: *Rustum is here!*
He will not yield indeed, nor quit our foes,
But he will find some pretext not to fight,
And praise my fame, and proffer courteous gifts,
A belt or sword perhaps, and go his way.
And on a feast-tide in Afrasiab's hall,
In Samarcand, he will arise and cry:
"I challenged once, when the two armies camp'd
Beside the Oxus, all the Persian lords
To cope with me in single fight: but they
Shrank; only Rustum dar'd; then he and I
Chang'd gifts, and went on equal terms away."
So will he speak, perhaps, while men applaud;
Then were the chiefs of Iran shamed through me.'
    And then he turn'd, and sternly spake aloud:—
'Rise! wherefore dost thou vainly question thus

Of Rustum? I am here, whom thou hast call'd
By challenge forth; make good thy vaunt, or yield!
Is it with Rustum only thou wouldst fight?
Rash boy, men look on Rustum's face and flee!
For well I know, that did great Rustum stand
Before thy face this day, and were reveal'd,
There would be then no talk of fighting more.
But being what I am, I tell thee this;
Do thou record it in thine inmost soul:
Either thou shalt renounce thy vaunt, and yield;
Or else thy bones shall strew this sand, till winds
Bleach them, or Oxus with his summer floods,
Oxus in summer wash them all away.'
     He spoke: and Sohrab answer'd, on his feet:—
'Art thou so fierce? Thou wilt not fright me so.
I am no girl, to be made pale by words.
Yet this thou hast said well, did Rustum stand
Here on this field, there were no fighting then.
But Rustum is far hence, and we stand here.
Begin: thou art more vast, more dread than I,
And thou art prov'd, I know, and I am young—
But yet Success sways with the breath of Heaven.
And though thou thinkest that thou knowest sure
Thy victory, yet thou canst not surely know.
For we are all, like swimmers in the sea,
Pois'd on the top of a huge wave of Fate,
Which hangs uncertain to which side to fall.
And whether it will heave us up to land,
Or whether it will roll us out to sea,
Back out to sea, to the deep waves of death,
We know not, and no search will make us know:
Only the event will teach us in its hour.'
     He spoke; and Rustum answer'd not, but hurl'd
His spear; down from the shoulder, down it came,

As on some partridge in the corn a hawk
That long has tower'd in the airy clouds
Drops like a plummet: Sohrab saw it come,
And sprang aside, quick as a flash: the spear
Hiss'd, and went quivering down into the sand
Which it sent flying wide:—then Sohrab threw
In turn, and full struck Rustum's shield: sharp rang,
The iron plates rang sharp, but turn'd the spear.
And Rustum seiz'd his club, which none but he
Could wield: an unlopp'd trunk it was, and huge,
Still rough; like those which men in treeless plains
To build them boats fish from the flooded rivers,
Hyphasis or Hydaspes, when, high up
By their dark springs, the wind in winter-time
Has made in Himalayan forests wrack,
And strewn the channels with torn boughs—so huge
The club which Rustum lifted now, and struck
One stroke; but again Sohrab sprang aside
Lithe as the glancing snake, and the club came
Thundering to earth, and leapt from Rustum's hand.
And Rustum follow'd his own blow, and fell
To his knees, and with his fingers clutch'd the sand:
And now might Sohrab have unsheath'd his sword,
And pierc'd the mighty Rustum while he lay
Dizzy, and on his knees, and chok'd with sand;
But he look'd on, and smil'd, nor bar'd his sword.
But courteously drew back, and spoke, and said:—

   'Thou strik'st too hard: that club of thine will float
Upon the summer floods, and not my bones.
But rise, and be not wroth; not wroth am I:
No, when I see thee, wrath forsakes my soul.
Thou say'st, thou art not Rustum: be it so!
Who art thou then, that canst so touch my soul?
Boy as I am, I have seen battles too;

Have waded foremost in their bloody waves,
And heard their hollow roar of dying men;
But never was my heart thus touch'd before.
Are they from Heaven, these softenings of the heart?
O thou old warrior, let us yield to Heaven!
Come, plant we here in earth our angry spears,
And make a truce, and sit upon this sand,
And pledge each other in red wine, like friends,
And thou shalt talk to me of Rustum's deeds.
There are enough foes in the Persian host
Whom I may meet, and strike, and feel no pang;
Champions enough Afrasiab has, whom thou
Mayst fight: fight them, when they confront thy spear.
But oh, let there be peace 'twixt thee and me!'
      He ceased: but while he spake, Rustum had risen,
And stood erect, trembling with rage: his club
He left to lie, but had regain'd his spear,
Whose fiery point now in his mail'd right hand
Blaz'd bright and baleful, like that autumn Star,
The baleful sign of fevers: dust had soil'd
His stately crest, and dimm'd his glittering arms.
His breast heav'd; his lips foam'd; and twice his voice
Was chok'd with rage: at last these words broke way:—
      'Girl! nimble with thy feet, not with thy hands!
Curl'd minion, dancer, coiner of sweet words!
Fight; let me hear thy hateful voice no more!
Thou art not in Afrasiab's gardens now
With Tartar girls, with whom thou art wont to dance;
But on the Oxus-sands, and in the dance
Of battle, and with me, who make no play
Of war: I fight it out, and hand to hand.
Speak not to me of truce, and pledge, and wine!
Remember all thy valour; try thy feints
And cunning: all the pity I had is gone;

Because thou hast sham'd me before both the hosts
With thy light skipping tricks, and thy girl's wiles.'
   He spoke; and Sohrab kindled at his taunts,
And he too drew his sword: at once they rush'd
Together, as two eagles on one prey
Come rushing down together from the clouds,
One from the east, one from the west: their shields
Dash'd with a clang together, and a din
Rose, such as that the sinewy woodcutters
Make often in the forest's heart at morn,
Of hewing axes, crashing trees—such blows
Rustum and Sohrab on each other hail'd.
And you would say that sun and stars took part
In that unnatural conflict; for a cloud
Grew suddenly in Heaven, and dark'd the sun
Over the fighters' heads; and a wind rose
Under their feet, and moaning swept the plain,
And in a sandy whirlwind wrapp'd the pair.
In gloom they twain were wrapp'd, and they alone;
For both the on-looking hosts on either hand
Stood in broad daylight, and the sky was pure,
And the sun sparkled on the Oxus stream.
But in the gloom they fought, with bloodshot eyes
And labouring breath; first Rustum struck the shield
Which Sohrab held stiff out: the steel-spik'd spear
Rent the tough plates, but fail'd to reach the skin,
And Rustum pluck'd it back with angry groan.
Then Sohrab with his sword smote Rustum's helm,
Nor clove its steel quite through; but all the crest
He shore away, and that proud horsehair plume,
Never till now defiled, sunk to the dust;
And Rustum bow'd his head; but then the gloom
Grew blacker: thunder rumbled in the air,
And lightnings rent the cloud; and Ruksh, the horse,

Who stood at hand, utter'd a dreadful cry:
No horse's cry was that, most like the roar
Of some pain'd desert lion, who all day
Has trail'd the hunter's javelin in his side,
And comes at night to die upon the sand.
The two hosts heard that cry, and quaked for fear,
And Oxus curdled as it cross'd his stream.
But Sohrab heard, and quail'd not, but rush'd on,
And struck again; and again Rustum bow'd
His head; but this time all the blade, like glass,
Sprang in a thousand shivers on the helm,
And in his hand the hilt remain'd alone.
Then Rustum rais'd his head: his dreadful eyes
Glar'd, and he shook on high his menacing spear,
And shouted, *Rustum!* Sohrab heard that shout,
And shrank amaz'd; back he recoil'd one step,
And scann'd with blinking eyes the advancing Form;
And then he stood bewilder'd; and he dropp'd
His covering shield, and the spear pierc'd his side.
He reel'd, and staggering back, sunk to the ground.
And then the gloom dispers'd, and the wind fell,
And the bright sun broke forth, and melted all
The cloud; and the two armies saw the pair;
Saw Rustum standing, safe upon his feet,
And Sohrab, wounded, on the bloody sand.
     Then, with a bitter smile, Rustum began:—
'Sohrab, thou thoughtest in thy mind to kill
A Persian lord this day, and strip his corpse,
And bear thy trophies to Afrasiab's tent.
Or else that the great Rustum would come down
Himself to fight, and that thy wiles would move
His heart to take a gift, and let thee go.
And then that all the Tartar host would praise
Thy courage or thy craft, and spread thy fame

To glad thy father in his weak old age.
Fool! thou art slain, and by an unknown man!
Dearer to the red jackals shalt thou be,
Than to thy friends, and to thy father old.'
    And, with a fearless mien Sohrab replied:—
'Unknown thou art; yet thy fierce vaunt is vain.
Thou dost not slay me, proud and boastful man!
No! Rustum slays me, and this filial heart.
For were I match'd with ten such men as thou,
And I were he who till to-day I was,
They should be lying here, I standing there.
But that belovèd name unnerv'd my arm—
That name, and something, I confess, in thee,
Which troubles all my heart, and made my shield
Fall; and thy spear transfix'd an unarm'd foe.
And now thou boastest, and insult'st my fate.
But hear thou this, fierce man, tremble to hear!
The mighty Rustum shall avenge my death!
My father, whom I seek through all the world,
He shall avenge my death, and punish thee!'
    As when some hunter in the spring hath found
A breeding eagle sitting on her nest,
Upon the craggy isle of a hill lake,
And pierced her with an arrow as she rose,
And follow'd her to find her where she fell
Far off;—anon her mate comes winging back
From hunting, and a great way off descries
His huddling young left sole; at that, he checks
His pinion, and with short uneasy sweeps
Circles above his eyry, with loud screams
Chiding his mate back to her nest; but she
Lies dying, with the arrow in her side,
In some far stony gorge out of his ken,
A heap of fluttering feathers—never more

Shall the lake glass her, flying over it;
Never the black and dripping precipices
Echo her stormy scream as she sails by:—
As that poor bird flies home, nor knows his loss,
So Rustum knew not his own loss, but stood
Over his dying son, and knew him not.

But with a cold, incredulous voice, he said:—
'What prate is this of fathers and revenge?
The mighty Rustum never had a son.'

And, with a failing voice, Sohrab replied:—
'Ah yes, he had! and that lost son am I.
Surely the news will one day reach his ear,
Reach Rustum, where he sits, and tarries long,
Somewhere, I know not where, but far from here;
And pierce him like a stab, and make him leap
To arms, and cry for vengeance upon thee.
Fierce Man, bethink thee, for an only son!
What will that grief, what will that vengeance be!
Oh, could I live, till I that grief had seen!
Yet him I pity not so much, but her,
My mother, who in Ader-baijan dwells
With that old King, her father, who grows grey
With age, and rules over the valiant Koords.
Her most I pity, who no more will see
Sohrab returning from the Tartar camp,
With spoils and honour, when the war is done.
But a dark rumour will be bruited up,
From tribe to tribe, until it reach her ear;
And then will that defenceless woman learn
That Sohrab will delight her sight no more;
But that in battle with a nameless foe,
By the far-distant Oxus, he was slain.'

He spoke; and as he ceas'd he wept aloud,
Thinking of her he left, and his own death.

He spoke; but Rustum listen'd, plung'd in thought.
Nor did he yet believe it was his son
Who spoke, although he call'd back names he knew;
For he had had sure tidings that the babe,
Which was in Ader-baijan born to him,
Had been a puny girl, no boy at all;
So that sad mother sent him word, for fear
Rustum should take the boy, to train in arms;
And so he deem'd that either Sohrab took,
By a false boast, the style of Rustum's son;
Or that men gave it him, to swell his fame.

     .   .   .   .   .   .

Piteous and lovely, lying on the sand,
Like some rich hyacinth, which by the scythe
Of an unskilful gardener has been cut,
Mowing the garden grass-plots near its bed,
And lies, a fragrant tower of purple bloom,
On the mown, dying grass;—so Sohrab lay,
Lovely in death, upon the common sand.
And Rustum gaz'd on him in grief, and said:—
   'O Sohrab, thou indeed art such a son
Who Rustum, wert thou his, might well have lov'd!
Yet here thou errest, Sohrab, or else men
Have told thee false; -thou art not Rustum's son.
For Rustum had no son: one child he had—
But one—a girl: who with her mother now
Plies some light female task, nor dreams of us—
Of us she dreams not, nor of wounds, nor war.'
   But Sohrab answer'd him in wrath; for now
The anguish of the deep-fix'd spear grew fierce,
And he desired to draw forth the steel,
And let the blood flow free, and so to die;
But first he would convince his stubborn foe—
And, rising sternly on one arm, he said:—

'Man, who art thou who dost deny my words?
Truth sits upon the lips of dying men,
And Falsehood, while I liv'd, was far from mine.
I tell thee, prick'd upon this arm I bear
That seal which Rustum to my mother gave,
That she might prick it on the babe she bore.'
    He spoke: and all the blood left Rustum's cheeks;
And his knees totter'd, and he smote his hand
Against his breast, his heavy mailed hand,
That the hard iron corslet clank'd aloud:
And to his heart he press'd the other hand,
And in a hollow voice he spake, and said:—
    'Sohrab, that were a proof which could not lie.
If thou show this, then art thou Rustum's son.'
    Then with weak hasty fingers, Sohrab loos'd
His belt, and near the shoulder bar'd his arm,
And shew'd a sign in faint vermilion points
Prick'd: as a cunning workman, in Pekin,
Pricks with vermilion some clear porcelain vase,
An emperor's gift—at early morn he paints,
And all day long, and, when night comes, the lamp
Lights up his studious forehead and thin hands:—
So delicately prick'd the sign appear'd
On Sohrab's arm, the sign of Rustum's seal.
It was that Griffin, which of old rear'd Zal,
Rustum's great father, whom they left to die,
A helpless babe, among the mountain rocks.
Him that kind Creature found, and rear'd, and lov'd—
Then Rustum took it for his glorious sign.
And Sohrab bar'd that figure on his arm,
And himself scann'd it long with mournful eyes,
And then he touch'd it with his hand, and said:—
    'How say'st thou? Is that sign the proper sign
Of Rustum's son, or of some other man's?'

169

He spoke: but Rustum gaz'd, and gaz'd, and stood
Speechless; and then he utter'd one sharp cry—
O Boy—thy Father! and his voice chok'd there.
And then a dark cloud pass'd before his eyes,
And his head swam, and he sunk down to earth.

. . . .

So, on the bloody sand, Sohrab lay dead.
And the great Rustum drew his horseman's cloak
Down o'er his face, and sate by his dead son.
As those black granite pillars, once high-rear'd
By Jemshid in Persepolis, to bear
His house, now, mid their broken flights of steps,
Lie prone, enormous, down the mountain side—
So in the sand lay Rustum by his son.
And night came down over the solemn waste,
And the two gazing hosts, and that sole pair,
And darken'd all: and a cold fog, with night,
Crept from the Oxus. Soon a hum arose,
As of a great assembly loos'd, and fires
Began to twinkle through the fog: for now
Both armies mov'd to camp, and took their meal:
The Persians took it on the open sands
Southward; the Tartars by the river marge:
And Rustum and his son were left alone.
But the majestic River floated on,
Out of the mist and hum of that low land,
Into the frosty starlight, and there mov'd,
Rejoicing, through the hush'd Chorasmian waste,
Under the solitary moon: he flow'd
Right for the Polar Star, past Orgunjè,
Brimming, and bright, and large: then sands begin
To hem his watery march, and dam his streams,
And split his currents; that for many a league
The shorn and parcell'd Oxus strains along

Through beds of sand and matted rushy isles—
Oxus, forgetting the bright speed he had
In his high mountain cradle in Pamere,
A foil'd circuitous wanderer:—till at last
The long'd-for dash of waves is heard, and wide
His luminous home of waters opens, bright
And tranquil, from whose floor the new-bath'd stars
Emerge, and shine upon the Aral Sea.

MATTHEW ARNOLD

79   *Requiem*

UNDER the wide and starry sky
    Dig the grave and let me lie:
Glad did I live and gladly die,
        And I laid me down with a will.

This be the verse you grave for me:
Here he lies where he long'd to be;
Home is the sailor, home from sea,
        And the hunter home from the hill.

R. L. STEVENSON

80   *The Spacious Firmament on High*

THE spacious firmament on high,
With all the blue ethereal sky,
And spangled heavens, a shining frame,
Their great Original proclaim.
Th' unwearied sun from day to day
Does his Creator's power display;
And publishes to every land
The work of an Almighty hand.

171

Soon as the evening shades prevail,
The Moon takes up the wondrous tale;
And nightly to the listening Earth
Repeats the story of her birth:
Whilst all the stars that round her burn,
And all the planets in their turn,
Confirm the tidings as they roll,
And spread the truth from pole to pole.

What though in solemn silence all
Move round the dark terrestrial ball;
What though no real voice nor sound
Amidst their radiant orbs be found?
In Reason's ear they all rejoice,
And utter forth a glorious voice;
For ever singing as they shine,
'The Hand that made us is divine.'

JOSEPH ADDISON

81   *Up-hill*

DOES the road wind up-hill all the way?
    Yes, to the very end.
Will the day's journey take the whole long day?
    From morn to night, my friend.

But is there for the night a resting-place?
    A roof for when the slow, dark hours begin.
May not the darkness hide it from my face?
    You cannot miss that inn.

172

Shall I meet other wayfarers at night?
  Those who have gone before.
Then must I knock, or call when just in sight?
  They will not keep you standing at that door.

Shall I find comfort, travel-sore and weak?
  Of labour you shall find the sum.
Will there be beds for me and all who seek?
  Yea, beds for all who come.
                    CHRISTINA ROSSETTI

82   *Jerusalem*

AND did those feet in ancient time
  Walk upon England's mountains green?
And was the holy Lamb of God
  On England's pleasant pasture seen?

And did the Countenance Divine
  Shine forth upon our clouded hills?
And was Jerusalem builded here
  Among these dark Satanic Mills?

Bring me my bow of burning gold!
  Bring me my arrows of desire!
Bring me my spear! O clouds, unfold!
  Bring me my chariot of fire!

I will not cease from mental fight,
  Nor shall my sword sleep in my hand,
Till we have built Jerusalem
  In England's green and pleasant land.
                    WILLIAM BLAKE

NOTES

The references are to the numbers of the poems

5. Oliver Goldsmith was born in Ireland. After a wandering life in which he tried several professions, he settled down in London as a writer of poems, essays, plays (e.g. *She Stoops to Conquer*) and a novel (*The Vicar of Wakefield*). In this poem he recalls the happy life in his native village before poverty caused so many of his fellow countrymen to emigrate. CYPHER: to calculate. GAUGE: to measure.

8. Julius Caesar, before becoming master of Rome, had a rival, Pompey, whom he finally defeated. In this poem the ghost of Pompey knocks at Caesar's door as he is sleeping fitfully on the eve of the Ides of March, the day of his assassination. CRESSETS: iron baskets or holders, for combustibles, as torches, &c. THE SANDS: Pompey was murdered in Egypt after fleeing from Caesar. LOANING: field or common.

9. This poem outlines the life story of Napoleon. It begins with his childhood in Corsica, and goes on to refer to his suppression of a rising in Paris in 1795. At the Battle of Austerlitz (1805) he triumphed over the combined armies of Europe. He had now assumed the title of Emperor of the French. The other places mentioned are his defeats, the naval battle of Trafalgar (1805), the River Beresina, where his army was destroyed after his disastrous retreat from Moscow (1812), and, finally, Waterloo (1815). He was banished to the Island of St. Helena, where he died in 1821.

12. Simon Legree was the cruel slave-owner, and Tom and Eva two slaves in the book, *Uncle Tom's Cabin*, which helped to arouse American opinion against the evil of slavery. Vachel Lindsay, an American, wrote many poems from a Negro point of view, e.g. *Daniel* (Book I) and *The Congo* (Book III). THE HIGH SANCTORIUMS: a quaint Negro expression for heaven. SHOOTING CRAPS: playing dice.

175

13, 14. These are ballads, a popular entertainment, when sung or re-
cited by wandering minstrels, up to the fifteenth century. The
subjects were sometimes imaginative like these, sometimes founded
on actual events like *Sir Patrick Spens* (Book I). Ballad metre consists
of stanzas of four lines of alternately eight and six syllables, with the
second and fourth lines rhyming. Often there is a chorus. LYKE-
WAKE: a watch over the dead.

15. A nineteenth-century imitation of the ballad, though the author has
taken liberties with the metre. It is based on the old belief that if one
made a wax image of an enemy and melted it before a fire, the subject
of the image would fade away and die. Here the story is told in
dialogue between the tragic Sister Helen, who is melting the image
of the man who has forsaken her, and the little brother, who looks
out of the window and sees the father, brother, and wife of the dying
man coming to plead for mercy.

16. Thomas Hood, an early nineteenth-century poet, wrote much light
verse. Here the fun arises from the use of puns, e.g. Nell–knell,
stake–steak, breaches–breeches. BADAJOS: a siege in the Peninsular
War (1808–14).

17. Sung by Feste, the Clown, in *Twelfth Night* (Act II, sc. iii).

18. ADRIAN'S MOLE: in Rome, built, as his tomb, by the Emperor
Hadrian, and now called the Castle of St. Angelo. THE VATICAN: the
home of the Pope. NOTRE DAME and ST. PETER'S: cathedrals in Paris
and Rome respectively. SANTA SOPHIA: the cathedral in Constanti-
nople, turned into a mosque by the Turks and now a museum.

23. Robert Herrick was vicar of a village on the edge of Dartmoor. His
religious poems were collected in a volume called *Noble Numbers*, his
more popular lighter ones in *Hesperides*. (See also No. 54.)

24. From *Saul*, in which Browning describes how the young David comes
to the ageing and despondent Saul, and by singing of the joyous
experiences of life puts fresh heart into the king.

25, 26. At the age of 34 Robert Browning eloped with Elizabeth
Barratt and lived in Italy for the next fifteen years. Yet he remembered
England with affection and was proud of her past glories. The places
mentioned in No. 26 are the scenes of English naval victories off

Cape St. Vincent there were victories by Rodney in 1780 and Jervis in 1797; Cadiz was where Drake 'singed the King of Spain's beard'; Trafalgar was the scene of Nelson's victory in 1805.

27. From *Richard II* (Act II, sc. i). John of Gaunt, Duke of Lancaster, speaks on his death-bed of the past glories of an England now being ruined by his frivolous nephew, King Richard II.

28. Not really a ballad but a *ballade*, a form of light verse in which there are three eight-line stanzas followed by an *Envoy* of four lines. Not more than three or four rhymes are used throughout, and the last line of each stanza and of the envoy is the same. CARRACKS: large ships for stores or war. KIRTLES: skirts. FLACCUS: Horace, a Latin poet. BACCHUS: the god of wine.

29. The Spanish Armada was first sighted off the Lizard on 19 July 1588, was harried up the Channel by the English fleet from Plymouth, and was eventually dispersed by a storm, only 50 ships of the original 149 returning to Spain. EDGECUMBE'S LOFTY HALL: Mount Edgecumbe, Plymouth. THE GAY LILIES: the fleur-de-lys, emblem of France. PICARD FIELD: Crecy, 1346, where Edward III and the Black Prince defeated an army including the King of Bohemia, whose plumes are still worn by the Prince of Wales, 15,000 Genoese crossbowmen, and the Emperor Charles IV of the Holy Roman Empire. AGINCOURT: Henry V defeated the French in 1415. SEMPER EADEM: 'always the same'. The personal standard of Elizabeth I. EDDYSTONE: a rock in Plymouth Bay. LYN: King's Lynn in Norfolk. ST. MICHAEL'S MOUNT: near Penzance. ELY'S STATELY FANE: Ely Cathedral. GAUNT'S EMBATTLED PILE: Lancaster Castle.

30. Sir Francis Drake died off Porto Bello in the West Indies in 1596 and was buried at sea.

34. *The Ancient Mariner* was Coleridge's main contribution to a book of poems, *Lyrical Ballads* (1798), composed jointly with Wordsworth as a result of their association while they were both living on the Quantock Hills in Somerset. The poem is basically a ballad, though there is much variation in the form.

35. LYONNESSE was a legendary land associated with King Arthur; it was thought to lie somewhere beyond Cornwall.

38. Written in the fifteenth century, and the oldest poem in this book. The language is known as Middle English.

39. From *In Memoriam*, in which Tennyson laments the death of Arthur Hallam, one of his Cambridge friends, who died when the poet was 24. The poem begins with utter grief, but ends, as this extract shows, on a note of hope.

42. A song from *As You Like It* (Act II, sc. v), in which a duke, banished from his court enjoys a free and easy life in the forest.

43. The setting is Exmoor, the stag-hunting district of Devon and Somerset. HARBOURED: tracked to covert. BROW, BAY AND TRAY: first, second and third antlers. BROCKET: a stag in its second year. BEAMED AND TINED: with stem and points. COOMB: a valley. SEVERN SEA: the Bristol Channel.

47. The life-story of the wild bull that roams the savannas or grassy plains of tropical America. Ralph Hodgson's poems show great sympathy for animals. (See *The Bells of Heaven*, Book I.)

48. From The Book of Job, chapter 39.

51. Much of Chesterton's poetry shows a love of medieval England and a dislike of modern civilization. The alliteration of the last lines is abandoned in the final stanza as he needed the name of a cemetery ('Kensal Green') to go with 'Paradise'.

52. Rudyard Kipling was born at Bombay, and, after school in England, returned there as a journalist from 1882 to 1889. Many of his poems are about soldiers in India and the East. He also wrote short stories about India, and a novel, *Kim*, the story of an English orphan boy who became involved in the Indian secret service. In this poem a soldier, now retired, remembers his time in Burma. THEBAW: a King of Burma. THE GREAT GOD BUDD: the God Buddha. HATHIS: elephants.

61. A complete story told in the short sentences used to describe the action of a play and called 'stage directions'.

62. From *Henry V* (Act III, sc. i). The king has invaded France, and after a repulse sweeps at the head of his troops into the town of Harfleur.

64. J. E. Flecker uses this song in his play, *Hassan* (see Book III), where it is sung by the Saracen bodyguard of the Caliph of Baghdad. INDUS

178

a river in Pakistan. STAMBOUL: Istambul (Constantinople). THE WATERS OF DESTINY: the Atlantic. SAMET: samite, heavy silk.

66. From *Barrack Room Ballads*. A marching song of the army in South Africa during the Boer War.

67. TARANTELLA: a lively dance originating in Italy but here given a Spanish setting. A good poem for reciting in chorus.

68. D. H. Lawrence's animal poems reflect his travels, e.g. *Snake* (Book III), Sicily, *Kangaroo* (Book IV), Australia, and *Mountain Lion*, Mexico. QUE TIENE, AMIGO? LEON—: what have you there, friend? A lion— HERMOSO ES!: you are beautiful, or what a beauty!

69. From *Cautionary Tales*, stories of bad children such as Matilda, who told lies, or Henry King, who chewed string. (See also *Lord Lundy*, Book III.)

70. Thomas Gray is best known as the author of *Elegy written in a Country Churchyard*. This, too, is an elegy or lament, but treated with mock seriousness. Eighteenth-century writers were fond of using classical allusions; hence: GENII OF THE STREAM: spirits of the river. NEREID: river nymph. TYRIAN HUE: a purple dye made from a shellfish at Tyre.

71. Robert Burns must have seen such an incident as he describes here, for he spent most of his life working on farms.

72, 73. Lewis Carroll, whose real name was Charles Lutwidge Dodgson, was a lecturer in mathematics at Oxford. He wrote the Alice books, in which these poems appear, to please a small girl he knew, Alice Liddell, daughter of Dean Liddell, part-author of the famous Greek Lexicon.

76. BHISTI: a water-carrier. HITHERAO: come here. PANEE LAO: bring water. JULDEE!: quickly! DOOLI: litter.

78. Some minor cuts have been made in this poem, but the essential story of the lost son remains, as do most of the long similes which are a feature of the poem. AFRASIAB: king of the nomad Tartars. KAI-KHOSROO: king of the Persians.

79. Robert Louis Stevenson wrote this epitaph for himself. It is carved on a stone high on the hill above Vailima, Samoa, in the South Seas, where he died.

82. SATANIC MILLS: perhaps a reference to the Industrial Revolution.

ANALYTICAL LIST OF POEMS

The numbers are those of the poems

BALLADS, 13, 14, 15, 16, 34, 57.

BIRDS AND BEASTS, 36, 43, 46, 47, 48, 56, 57, 58, 59, 60, 68, 70, 71, 72, 73.

DRAMATIC, 27, 61, 62.

HISTORY, 8, 9, 29, 30, 62.

HUMOUR, 12, 17, 45, 46, 69, 70, 74, 75.

LAMENTS, 13, 21, 70, 79.

NARRATIVE, 6, 15, 29, 33, 34, 47, 50, 76, 77, 78.

OPEN AIR, 20, 24, 41, 42, 43, 44, 51, 53.

PATRIOTISM, 25, 26, 27, 28, 29, 30.

PEOPLE, 5, 6, 9, 11, 12, 14, 41, 45, 50, 75, 76.

PLACES, 2, 3, 4, 5, 18, 32, 35, 52.

POEMS SUITABLE FOR CHORAL SPEAKING, 12, 13, 18, 28, 30, 48, 64, 66, 67.

RELIGION, 38, 80, 81, 82.

RHYTHM AND MOVEMENT, 49, 51, 65, 66, 67.

SEA, 21, 22, 30, 31, 37.

SEASONS, 36, 37, 38, 39, 40, 55.

SUPERNATURAL, 8, 12, 13, 15, 33, 34.

WAR, 63, 64, 66.

CHRONOLOGICAL LIST OF AUTHORS

The poets are placed in the period of their greatest poetic activity. The numbers in brackets are those of the poems.

EARLY POEMS. Ballads (13, 14, 57); Carol (38).

LATE SIXTEENTH CENTURY AND EARLY SEVENTEENTH CENTURY. The Bible (48); T. Dekker (7); R. Herrick (23, 54); T. Nashe (55); W. Shakespeare (17, 27, 42, 62); H. Wotton (10).

EIGHTEENTH CENTURY. J. Addison (80); R. Burns (44, 71), O. Goldsmith (5). T. Gray (70),

NINETEENTH CENTURY.

   i. W. Blake (73, 82); S. T. Coleridge (34); T. Hood (16); W. Wordsworth (58).

  ii. J. Clare (41); Lord Macaulay (29); F. Mahony (18); T. L. Peacock (63).

 iii. M. Arnold (78); R. Browning (24, 25, 26); L Carroll (74, 75); A. Dobson (28); C. Kingsley (22); W. Morris (77); C. Rossetti (81); D. Rossetti (15); R. L. Stevenson (37, 79); Lord Tennyson (19, 20, 21, 39).

TWENTIETH CENTURY. M. Armstrong (6); H. Belloc (46, 67, 69); W. R. Benet (61); R. Brooke (1); G. K. Chesterton (51); J. Davidson (43); W. H. Davies (59); W. de la Mare (72); J. E. Flecker (64); W. Gibson (4, 33); H. Graham (45); T. Hardy (35, 36); R. Hodgson (47); R. Kipling (9, 52, 53, 66, 76); D. H. Lawrence (68); V. Lindsay (12); J. Masefield (8, 32, 60); H. Newbolt (30, 31); A. Noyes (50); W. H. Ogilvie (49); O. Sitwell (40); C. Sorley (65); J. C. Squire (11); J. Stephens (56); E. Thomas (2); W. B. Yeats (3).

INDEX OF AUTHORS AND TITLES

INDEX OF FIRST LINES

PRINTED IN GREAT BRITAIN
AT THE UNIVERSITY PRESS, OXFORD
BY VIVIAN RIDLER
PRINTER TO THE UNIVERSITY